Debates
with Devils

Debates with Devils

What Swedenborg Heard in Hell

Donald L. Rose

Translated by Lisa Hyatt Cooper
With an Introduction
by Leonard Fox

CHRYSALIS BOOKS

WEST CHESTER, PENNSYLVANIA

Library of Congress Cataloging-in-Publication Data

Swedenborg, Emanuel, 1688-1772.
    [Essays. English. Selections]
    Debates with devils : what Swedenborg heard in hell / Donald L. Rose, author [i.e. editor] ; Lisa Hyatt Cooper, translator ; with an introduction by Leonard Fox.
        p. cm.
     ISBN 0-87785-385-1
     1. Hell. 2. Demonology. I. Rose, Donald L. II. Title.
BX8729.H5 S94213 2000
289.4—dc21

                                                                00-031572

Cover and text design by C. Mayapriya Long, www.bookwrights.com
Set in Berkeley Oldstyle by Bookwrights Design
Printed in the United States of America

Credits: Excerpt from *J.B.* Copyright ©1956, 1957, 1958 by Archibald MacLeish. Copyright (c) renewed 1986 by William H. MacLeish and Mary H. Grimm. Reprinted by permission of Houghton Mifflin Company.

For more information on Swedenborg Foundation Publishers, contact:
    Swedenborg Foundation
    320 North Church Street
    West Chester, PA 19380
    or http://www.swedenborg.com.

Contents

Introduction

by Leonard Fox

Unde malum? — From whence evil?

In his work *J.B.*, an adaptation of the Book of Job as a play in verse, the poet Archibald MacLeish summed up in two lines the primary theological dilemma of millennia of monotheistic religion:

> If God is God He is not good,
> If God is good He is not God.[1]

In the West, the first recorded formulation of this dilemma was made by the Greek philosopher Epicurus (341–270 B.C.E.). As quoted by the third-century Church Father Lactantius, in his work *De Ira Dei* (On the Anger of God), it runs as follows:

> God either wishes to take away evils, and is unable; or He is able and is unwilling; or He is neither willing nor able, or He is both willing and able. If He is willing and is unable, He is feeble, which is not in accordance with the character of God; if He is able and unwilling, He is envious, which is equally at variance with God; if He is neither willing nor able, He is both envious and feeble, and therefore not God; if He is both willing and able, which alone is suitable to God, from what source then are evils? or why does He not remove them?[2]

The theological term that is used for the subject of attempting to resolve the problem of evil is *theodicy*, from the Greek θεός, "God," and δίκη justice." Theodicy involves defending the justice, righteousness, goodness, and love of God in the face of the existence of evil.

Zoroastrian Theodicy

Historically, the first recorded monotheistic religion is Zoroastrianism. Its founder, Zarathushtra (or Zoroaster, as he was called in Greek), lived sometime between 1200 and 1500 B.C.E. Although Zoroastrianism is generally represented by writers on religion as exemplifying a theology of *dualism*—the concept that there are two primordial, coexistent, and coequal principles, one of good and the other of evil—this is not, in fact, the theology that is found in the Gāthās, the oldest Zoroastrian scriptures, said to be by Zarathushtra himself. It is, rather, a much later development in the religion—the moral dualism taught in the earliest times having gradually become a cosmic dualism embodied in a complex mythological drama. The protagonists are pitted against one another in an ongoing struggle for supremacy in the universe, although there is a foregone conclusion that good will triumph at the end of time.

It is worthwhile outlining here the Zoroastrian approach to theodicy, in view of the fact that, as A. V. Williams Jackson has written,

> Anyone who has even a superficial knowledge of the Iranian religion cannot but be struck by the parallels that may be drawn between it on the one hand and Judaism and Christianity on the other. The ideas of God, angels and archangels, of Devil, demons and archfiends, as found in both, present so great a similarity that comparisons between the angelology and demonology of the two types of religion become inevitable.[3]

It has been recognized by many other scholars, as well, that Zoroastrianism had a significant impact on Judaism, and through Judaism on both Christianity and Islam. We will also find that many of the essential elements of Zoroastrian theodicy are present in Swedenborg's theological writings, although there can be no question here of influence, since the Zoroastrian sacred scriptures had not yet been translated during the period of Swedenborg's lifetime.

The theology of the Gāthās is uncompromisingly monotheistic. God, Ahura Mazda, is conceived to be the infinite and eternal Ultimate Reality, both transcendent and immanent. In his transcendence, he cannot be grasped by human finite intellect; but in his immanence, he manifests himself to mankind in his attributes: the Zoroastrian tradition mentions 101 of these, but primary among them are love, wisdom, goodness, truth, righteousness and justice, omniscience, omnipotence, omnipresence, perfection, and immutability.

Zoroastrianism teaches that, in creating mankind, Ahura Mazda endowed the human being with free will. Indeed, man's spiritual freedom is considered to be a component of the divine order and law, since the religion views the human being as God's collaborator in the perfecting of creation. The divine gift of free will is the source of the moral dualism that lies at the heart of the Zoroastrian religion. This form of dualism can be understood as a mental phenomenon, a behavioral attitude that conditions the choices of how an individual will think and act. On the one hand, moral dualism relates to the principle of freedom of choice; on the other hand, it relates to the law of consequences—of reward and punishment. Once again, the question needs to be asked, "From whence evil?" In Zoroastrian doctrine, there is no concept of original sin. When humankind first appeared on earth, two forms of mentality came into existence spontaneously within the species—one good, the other evil. Humanity's freedom of choice presupposes alternatives, and these two mentalities represent two alternate courses of action that people are at liberty to follow.

The Gāthās call evil the "non-good" (a concept restated in some of the early Christian writers). Goodness in creation cannot be perceived without its opposite. Good and evil in this world, therefore, become matters of function, and not substance. They do not have substance outside the realm of human thought, speech, and action. Goodness on our plane of existence is a reflection of the absolute goodness of the Divine; but since evil has no relation to the transcendent Divine, it is only in the world of relativity, in the creation of a free human being, that it can manifest itself through free human choice. When an individual makes the incorrect choice, he or she creates and activates evil within himself and society. Evil, then, is not something outside of human beings, but is an internal element that we can choose to reject or accept. It can be said, then, that if every human being made the right choices in life, there would be no evil.

Zoroastrian theodicy resolves the problem of evil by saying that it is not God, but humankind who creates evil. God created people not as a slave or a puppet, but as spiritually free beings, fully responsible for—and liable to the consequences of—their choices. As perfection itself, God could not originate an imperfect creation. The imperfection of evil, therefore, was introduced into creation by humanity.

Jewish Theodicy

In the second chapter of Genesis, after God had completed his creation of the universe and all that was in it, including human beings, it is stated: "Then God saw everything that He had made, and indeed it was very good" (v. 31). Evil, in the form of sin, arises in the third chapter, when Adam and Eve eat the fruit of the tree of the knowledge of good and evil, which had been forbidden to them. When God questions Adam about his disobedience, Adam attempts to justify himself by ascribing the cause of evil to God: "The woman whom You gave to be with me, she gave me of the tree, and I ate" (3:12). Eve, too, tries to blame their act on an external cause connected with God's creation: "The serpent deceived me, and I ate" (3:13). In fact, however, there is no causal connection between the creation and the first appearance of evil, just as the text of Genesis does not indicate any causal connection between the first sin and those which follow, such as the murder of Abel by his brother Cain.

In his exegesis of chapters two and three of Genesis, in the first part of his extensive study of evil, the German theologian Eugen Drewermann comments that, when humanity alienated itself from God through sin, a new meaning was given to the human state, which was now able to transform God's blessings into punishments. Sin contains its own punishment within itself, because when it obtains its desired or intended goal, it transforms it into its opposite. Sin is an *orientation* within humanity, but one for which humanity is, at the same time, responsible.[4] More than two centuries earlier, Swedenborg wrote in *Divine Providence* 249: "Its own punishment follows every evil; it is as if its punishment were inscribed upon the evil." In another work, *Heaven and Hell,* he wrote, "Whoever is in evil is also in the punishment of evil"(§ 509).

In the text of the Old Testament as a whole, and in the noncanonical books of the Apocrypha, though, there is an obvious tension that is seen between the passages that, so to speak, absolve God from any direct connection with the origin of evil and those that seem to imply that God, as the sole source of everything in created life, is, in some way, also the source of evil. Some examples of this latter viewpoint are: "I am the Lord, and there is no other; I form the light and create darkness, I make peace and create evil" ['evil,' 'distress,' 'misery,' 'calamity,' and 'adversity,' translated in the Septuagint as κακά]; I, the Lord, do all these things" (Isaiah 45:6–7); "If there is evil in a city, will not the Lord have done it?" (Amos 3:6); "Shall we receive good from God and not receive evil?" (Job 2:10); "Then God sent an evil spirit between Abimelech and the men of Shechem" (Judges 9:23); "But the Spirit of the Lord departed from Saul, and an evil spirit from the Lord troubled him" (1 Samuel 16:14).

In considering these and similar statements, Swedenborg draws an important distinction between genuine truths and apparent truths in the Bible. A *genuine* truth, truly reflective of the divine nature is one such as "The Lord is good to all, and His tender mercies are over all His works" (Psalm 145:9), whereas when God is said to be angry or vengeful or to originate evil, these are apparent truths—apparent because they *appeared* to be true to the ancient Israelites, whose perceptions were based upon their own nature, rather than on the qualities of God. However, as Herbert Haag has pointed out, the Judaism of the Old Testament understood, too, that all the actions of God have goodness and salvation as their goal, and that the "evil" ascribed to God, in the sense of adversities or judgments, is permitted because of its positive purpose.[5] Even in the case of Job, the afflictions he was permitted to undergo brought him to a more profound understanding of the Divine.

It is in Ecclesiastes and especially in the Hebrew Apocrypha that we encounter the most uncompromising statements about the human origin of evil: "Truly, this only I have found: that God made man upright, but they have sought out many schemes" (Ecclesiastes 7:29); "Say not: 'It was God's doing that I fell away'; for what He hates He does not do. Say not: 'It was He who set me astray'; for He has no need of wicked man. Abominable wickedness the Lord hates, He does not let it befall those who fear Him. When God, in the beginning, created man, He made him subject to his own free choice. . . . Before man are life and death, whichever he chooses shall be given him" (Sirach 15:11–14, 17).

As Judaism developed in the postbiblical era, the issue of theodicy was given greater emphasis. In their efforts to resolve the problem of evil, the rabbis of the Talmudic period taught that the human will is not unified, but is divided between an inclination to good and an inclination to sin, or evil. The latter is mentioned in the eighth chapter of Genesis, where God says, "the inclination of man's heart is evil from his youth" (v. 21). But if God created man with an inclination to evil, is he not to some degree responsible for its results? Being committed to the belief in the absolute goodness of God, the rabbis said that there must be a good reason for the existence of an evil inclination—in fact, that it serves some divine purpose. They reasoned, therefore, that this inclination is not intrinsically evil, but may be used by a person in various ways, since he or she has been given free will. Sexuality, for example, may be a cause for sin, but it can also be directed to the positive purpose of having a family. The Talmud teaches that the evil inclination cannot be overcome by the individual. Although it was created by God, the weapon to fight against it was also given by God in the form of the Torah. It is only with God's help that the innate human attraction to evil can be resisted.

In the Middle Ages, Jewish philosopher-theologians such as Maimonides and Abraham ben David Halevi viewed the question of evil primarily from the standpoint of the limitations in the created universe. God, they said, cannot do what is impossible within the framework of his own order. He cannot, for example, make one number equal another without adding or subtracting something. Four always equals four; it cannot equal five without adding one. Similarly, God could not give humankind free will and the ability to choose good and reject evil if evil did not exist, making choice impossible. Halevi, writing under the influence of Plotinus and other Neoplatonic philosophers, taught that evil as such has no true reality, no being; it is actually the absence or privation of good, just as darkness is the absence of light. In the same philosophical tradition, the origins of which are to be found in Plato, Maimonides says that the creation of a material universe must also include the properties of privation, since matter must have this property in order to be matter. On the individual personal level, however, from Maimonides' point of view, it is only in a world where human beings have the freedom to fight against domination by evil within themselves that they can attain to spiritual, moral, and ethical worthiness.

The *Zohar*, the central work of Kabbalah, the Jewish mystical tradition, which dates from the thirteenth century C.E., explains the origin of evil in the Genesis story in a highly graphic manner. It says that all manifestation emanates from the same unmanifest, transcendent source, the *Eyn Sof*, the Infinite, which is unknowable and inexpressible. Everything that exists, therefore, is an aspect of God, and humanity, being the image and likeness of God, was created to replicate his attributes on a finite level. These attributes occur as an interconnected series of divine potencies, called *sefirot*, which is symbolized as the tree of life. The sin committed by Adam, which resulted in the origin of evil, was not disobedience to an external rule, but a spiritual misperception. Instead of seeing the reality of the tree of life—that is., the complete interconnectedness of existence as a unified divine system—Adam focused only on the appearances of manifestation, the tree of the knowledge of good and evil. In seeing himself as separate from the divine harmony, his internal microcosmic tree—the image and likeness of God—was broken. The break in his consciousness caused a break in his relationship with the macrocosmic consciousness represented by the union of the sefirot. From the perspective of the Kabbalah, evil is not nonbeing; it occurs as the result of a rupture in the connections between the *sefirot*, especially between *chesed* and *din*—love and justice—since justice without love gives rise to suffering, hatred, and other negative phenomena. In order to overcome evil, the task of every person is to heal that rupture within himself or herself, so that he or she may become a vessel receptive of the outpouring of the divine flow in its unified completeness. We then become reflections of the macrocosm and are able to reflect its unity back to the cosmos as a whole.

It may be noted parenthetically that in the structure of Swedenborg's theology, great emphasis is given to the necessity of linkage between the goodness of love and the truth of faith:

> Truth without good is not truth; that there may be truth it must be conjoined to good, and that there may be good it must be conjoined to truth. There may be indeed truth without good and good without truth; but truth without good is dead, and so is good without truth. For truth has its being from good, and good has its existence by means of truth. . . . Where there is no good of love there is evil. *Apocalypse Explained* 1008–1009

New Testament Theodicy

The theme of the New Testament in its entirety may be characterized as the struggle between good and evil, personified on the one hand by Jesus Christ and on the other by Satan. The number of references to Satan, Beelzebub, the devil, demons, and evil or unclean spirits in the Gospels, Revelation, and the Pauline Epistles, in comparison to the entire Old Testament (excluding the book of Job), is in a ratio of about twenty to one. The striking preoccupation with supernatural embodiments of evil almost reaches the level of cosmic dualism in the Gospel of John, where we read that the devil "was a murderer from the beginning, and does not stand in truth, because there is no truth in him. When he speaks a lie, he speaks from his own resources, for he is a liar and the father of it" (8:44). While Jesus, the divine Logos, was *in* the beginning, the devil has existed *from* the beginning. Although not as extreme in its dualism, in some respects this is reminiscent of the late Zoroastrian idea that Ohrmazd (the Ahura Mazda of the Gāthās) engendered Spenta Mainyu, the spirit of goodness, and Angra Mainyu, the spirit of evil. In the Gospel of John, the devil is "the ruler of this world" (12:31), and human beings are his children: "You are of your father the devil, and the desires of your father you want to do" (8:44). In this Johannine view, the direct cause of evil is a spiritual being operating independently of both God and man. It is possible to see here the culmination of a theodical perspective that begins in the third chapter of Genesis, undergoes the influence of Zoroastrianism, as well as the dualist thought of the Qumran community (whose doctrines, as presented in the Dead Sea Scrolls, posited that the world is divided equally between two spirits—the Prince of Light and the Angel of Darkness), and is reinforced by Gnostic currents. The Protestant theologian Rudolf Bultmann has written that "the cosmological dualism of Gnosticism has become in John a dualism of decision,"[6] where each individual is confronted with deciding for or against God.

That there is an entire dimension of spirits of varying degrees of evil is also stated in the synoptic Gospels: "When an unclean spirit goes out of a man, he goes through dry places, seeking rest, and finds none. Then he says, 'I will return to my house from which I came.' . . . Then he goes and takes with him seven other spirits more wicked than himself, and they enter and dwell there" (Matthew 12:43–45; cf. Luke 11:24–26). Despite this concept of evil as an entity outside of man, Jesus makes it clear that it is the evil inclination of the human spirit which bears the responsibility for the evil that a person does: "What comes out of a man, that defiles a man. For from within, out of the heart of men, proceed evil thoughts, adulteries, fornications, murders, thefts, covetousness, wickedness, deceit, lewdness, an evil eye, blasphemy, pride, foolishness. All these evil things come from within and defile a man" (Mark 7:20–23); "A good man out of the good treasure of his heart brings forth good things, and an evil man out of the evil treasure brings forth evil things" (Matthew 12:35).

Gnostic Theodicy

Gnosticism, while not a unified religion, but rather a number of belief systems having certain basic theological concepts in common, was in serious competition with the developing Christian Church during its first three centuries. An essential element of Gnostic belief was the irreconcilable dualism of the physical and the spiritual. The world and the flesh were considered to be evil, and, as Plato also taught, the soul was thought to be the true human essence that is temporarily imprisoned in the corrupt material form of the body. In the Gnostic Gospel of Thomas, Jesus says: "How miserable is the body that depends on a body, and how miserable is the soul that depends on these two" (logion 87).

Many Gnostics rejected the Old Testament, seeing it as portraying not the true God, but a demiurge who created the physical world in the image of his own evil. According to Basilides, the earliest known Gnostic writer, the true God manifested himself in Jesus Christ in order to reveal himself to those who are truly human, that is, who are spiritual rather than attached to their transient physicality. The knowledge (*gnosis*) of God is what brings humans to the remembrance of their divine origin and frees them from the captivity of matter, so that they can reject the world, separate themselves from it, and, now purified, follow the path on which they will return to the spiritual kingdom of God.

Manichaean Theodicy

The Iranian prophet Mani, the founder of Manichaeism, was born in Mesopotamia in 216 C.E. He had a revelatory experience in his early youth, and, at the age of twenty-four, said that an angel had commanded him to begin preaching the true religion for all mankind. Mani considered himself to be the Apostle of Light, the embodiment of the Paraclete promised in the Gospel of John, where Jesus says: "The Helper, the Holy Spirit, whom the Father will send in My name, He will teach you all things, and bring to your remembrance all things that I said to you" (14:26).

Mani taught a syncretistic religion that combined elements of

Zoroastrianism, Judaism, Christianity, Gnosticism, and Buddhism. He envisioned this faith as a universal one, and, indeed, the missionary efforts of his followers brought Manichaeism to all parts of the known world, including the Middle East, North Africa, Central Asia (where Manichaeism was the official religion of the Uighur kingdom), and China. Although some scholars have doubted a direct influence, it seems certainly possible that after maintaining an underground presence through centuries of persecution by Zoroastrians, Christians, and Muslims, Manichaeism resurfaced, albeit in more simplifled forms of both absolute and modified dualism, in the medieval Paulicians of Armenia, Bogomils of Bulgaria, and, most importantly, the Cathars of France, Italy, and Germany, who were annihilated by the Inquisition and the Catholic-sponsored Albigensian Crusade.

The foundation of Manichaean belief was a modified dualism: God, called Ohrmazd (the Middle Persian form of Ahura Mazda), is the source of all goodness, symbolized by light. Matter is intrinsically evil; it was called into existence by Ahriman, the personification of the principle of evil, ruler of the kingdom of darkness. Manichaean mythology is highly complex; but suffice it to say that in this system, although Adam and Eve are conceived of initially as demons, human beings have, mixed within the darkness of matter that constitutes their physical bodies, elements of light that form their soul: as one of the major Manichaean texts says, "Good and evil dwell in every person." The process of liberating the divine light, so that it may return to God, is lengthy and difficult, and, in the case of those who are not altogether righteous, may take several lifetimes, hence the Manichaean doctrine of reincarnation.

Manichaeism was a very appealing religion for many people in the ancient world and was a significant rival to Christianity in a number of geographical areas. The pacifism that was an important element of its doctrine was certainly one of the major reasons for its extinction, since its adherents would not defend themselves against the armed assaults of an aggressive Christian Church that would not tolerate any opposition to the spread of what it construed to be the only true faith.

Among those who were attracted to Manichaeism was St. Augustine, who found its dualist worldview an intellectually satisfying answer to the problem of evil, and who remained a Manichaean for almost ten years.

Christian Theodicy

In 386, at the age of thirty-two, and approximately a year after he had left the Manichaeans—a year in which he had devoted himself to studying the works of Plotinus and other Neoplatonic philosophers—St. Augustine first treated the problem of evil in a work entitled *De Ordine* (On Order). In this book, Augustine takes the Neoplatonic position that the origin of evil is in nonbeing. In his *Enneads*, Plotinus says:

> If [evil] exists, it must be among non-existent things, as a kind of form of non-existence, and pertain to one of the things that are mingled with non-being or share in non-being. Non-being here does not mean absolute non-being, but only something other than

being; not non-being in the same way as the movement and rest that affect being, but like an image of being or something still more non-existent. (I.8.3)

God could not be the source of evil, because, according to Augustine, no positive reality exists outside of divine providence. In his later works, Augustine develops the idea of the essential nonexistence of evil. In his *City of God* (XI.22), he says specifically that there is no "natural evil," that is, whatever exists is good, and there is nothing whose "nature" is evil, since all natures were created by God, and God can only create what is good (a theme that recurs in his *Nature of the Good*). In his attempts to refute the Manichaean doctrine of dualism, Augustine even states that, because the devil is a creature, a created entity, the devil's nature is also good! According to this author, nothing is by nature intrinsically evil. What may appear to us as evil—natural phenomena such as hurricanes, forest fires, and the like, for example—are good in their own natures, although we perceive them as harmful. If we experience suffering from the effects of these phenomena, that suffering is actually a punishment from God for the sins we have committed, and is therefore just. The things that cause us suffering are necessarily useful for our spiritual existence, and so are instrumentally good.

For Augustine, the only real evil is moral evil—sin. Sin occurs when we misuse the free will given to us by God (we could not live as humans without free will, he says). Evil, as sin, consists in turning away from God, who is unchanging goodness, truth, and wisdom.[8] But is even sin a genuine evil? In fact, Augustine considers that sin is only an apparent evil. In many places in his books, Augustine reiterates his belief that God permitted evil because he could bring good out of it. He argues that apparent evil is more than compensated for by the good that results from it, so, in effect, evil itself is instrumentally good. God is always able to use the human evil of sin for good purposes: "The universe is beautified even by sinners, though, considered by themselves, their deformity is a sad blemish" (*City of God*, XI.23); "God judged it better to bring good out of evil than not to permit any evil to exist" (*Enchiridion*, VIII.27); "If it were not good that evil things exist, they would certainly not be allowed to exist by the Omnipotent Good" (ibid., XXIV.96).

Augustine's theodicy, then, can be summarized in the conclusion he reaches throughout his works, from the earliest to the last, namely, that despite human perceptions and the appearances we judge by, there is, in reality, no genuine evil as such.

Another early Christian writer who dealt with the problem of evil was Pseudo-Dionysius, who claimed in his writings to be the first-century Athenian Dionysius the Areopagite, mentioned in the Book of Acts (17:34) as one of Paul's converts. In fact, the books written by this anonymous author have been dated to the end of the fifth century. These works, which Thomas Aquinas called "the peak of the human knowledge of God," were of extraordinary importance as a vehicle that transmitted Neoplatonic thought and infused it into Christianity. For more than a thousand years, Pseudo-Dionysius remained one of the principal influences on

Christian theology, strongly affecting such major thinkers and
mystics as John Eriugena and Meister Eckhart.

In his work *The Divine Names*, Dionysius says that there is
nothing in the world that does not have a share of the Beautiful
and the Good. Evil, however, does not come from the Good. But if
that is so, what is the origin of evil—and what is evil? As a
Neoplatonist, he begins his reply to this question in terms similar
to the passage from Plotinus quoted above:

> Evil is not a being; for if it were, it would not be totally evil. Nor is
> it a non-being; for nothing is completely a nonbeing, unless it is
> said to be in the Good in the sense of beyond-being. For the Good
> is established far beyond and before simple being and nonbeing.
> Evil, by contrast, is not among the things that have being, nor is it
> among what is not in being. It has a greater nonexistence and
> otherness from the Good than nonbeing has.[9]

In this last sentence, it appears as though Dionysius is propos-
ing a kind of Gnostic or Manichaean dualism, but he goes on to
say that in a negative sense, evil is connected to the Good; in a
positive sense, evil is understood to be a lesser good:

> A lesser good is not the opposite of the greater good. What is less
> hot or cold is not the opposite of what is more so. Therefore, evil is
> a being. It is in things that have being. And it is in opposition to
> and contrary to the Good.[10]

As an aspect of being, then, evil is a lesser good. It is positive
in the sense that it occurs in the creative processes of emanation

from the Good—a core teaching of Neoplatonism. These processes emerge in a hierarchical series of beings that participate in the Good *in proportion to the capacity to receive it*[11] (emphasized here because of the importance Swedenborg gives to the concept of reception of good and evil). As a lesser good, Dionysius justifies the existence of evil by saying that it "contributes to the fulfillment of the world and by its very existence it saves it from imperfection."[12]

Evil in itself, though, can be viewed as totally removed from the Good. In that case, it has no being, no existence, since only in some sort of relationship to the Good can it have force or life. In connection with the reality of the nonexistence of evil *qua* evil, Dionysius makes an interesting observation about demons:

> They are called evil because of the deprivation, the abandonment, the rejection of the virtues which are appropriate to them. And they are evil to the extent that they are not, and insofar as they wish for evil, they wish for what is really not there.[13]

For Dionysius, existence means participation, even in the smallest degree, in the Good. In that sense, even the most abominably evil beings are minimally good because they exist. Their reception of evil, however, brings them into a state that moves them to the very edge of existence—to annihilation and emptiness.

Parallel with Augustinian and Dionysian theodicy, another stream of thought originated in the Eastern Church with Irenaeus, Bishop of Lyons (ca. 140–ca. 200), and other Hellenistic Church Fathers of the second and third centuries. In the Western world,

Irenaeus has been best known for his five treatises "Against Heresies." In recent decades, however, it is Irenaeus' theodical ideas that have generated great interest among theologians, primarily because of John Hick's now classic work on the problem of evil, *Evil and the God of Love.*

Irenaeus, rather than regarding humanity as created in a perfect state from which it fell (a position held by Augustine, Aquinas, and the theologians of the Western Christian tradition in general, whether Catholic or Protestant), viewed man as still in the process of creation. Moral evil, sin, according to him, is an inevitable result of God having created the human being as an incomplete creature, a being only at the beginning of a lengthy process of spiritual development. This concept is called the "soul-making" theodicy, and it postulates that positive and valuable human qualities cannot be fully developed without subjecting man to suffering and challenge.

At the end of his book, Hick summarizes the Irenaean position as follows:

> The main features of Irenaean theodicy stress the creation of man, through the processes of natural evolution, at an epistemic distance from God, giving him a basic freedom in relation to his Creator; and man's consequent self-centeredness as an animal organism seeking survival within a harsh and challenging world which is however an environment in which he can develop, as a morally and spiritually immature creature, towards his ultimate perfection; this development beginning in the present life and continuing far beyond it. Such a theodicy sees moral and natural evil as necessary

features of the present stage of God's creating of perfected finite persons, although the precise forms which they have taken are of course contingent. Thus the ultimate responsibility for the existence of evil belongs to the Creator; and Christianity also believes that, in His total awareness of the history of His creation, God bears with us the pains of His creative process.[14]

A critique of Irenaean theodicy as interpreted by Hick is outside the scope of this introduction, but it is evident that this theodical viewpoint leaves a great many metaphysical questions unanswered. It might be suggested that the popularity of Hick's work among contemporary writers on theology accords with the current moral and ethical climate of Western society, in which abdication of personal responsibility for the evils that one commits has become a pandemic phenomenon.

Swedenborgian Theodicy

In his theological writings, Emanuel Swedenborg examines the problem of evil frequently and in great detail. The crucial issues of theodicy are dealt with in a manner that is both spiritually and intellectually authoritative. In order to present an overview of Swedenborg's theodical doctrines, an attempt will be made here to give the gist of his responses to the three fundamental questions about evil that are involved in every consideration of the subject:

1. What is evil?
2. From whence is evil?
3. Why does God permit evil?

What is Evil?

We have seen in earlier theodical thought that this question has been answered in several different ways, ranging from the dualist response that evil is a primordial spiritual force in the universe to Augustine's negation of its very existence. In a passage dated 1748 in his *Spiritual Diary* 3939, Swedenborg says: " To be nothing signifies to be nothing but evil, for evil is in itself death; wherefore compared to life it is nothing. That the good and the true is everything, is plain, wherefore the evil and the false is nothing." In his later writings, Swedenborg qualifies and explains this view, for example, in *Divine Providence* 19: "What is in goodness and at the same time in truth has reality; and from this it follows that what is evil and at the same time false has no reality. By having no reality is meant that it has no power and no spiritual life."

The kabbalistic concept, that evil constitutes a break in the unity of the sefirotic nexus of the cosmic macrocosm as it is reflected in the consciousness of the human microcosm, is echoed in Swedenborg's *Arcana Cœlestia*, section 4997: "Regarded in itself, evil, and also sin, is nothing else than disjunction from good. Moreover, evil itself consists in disunion," and also in section 5746: "Evil is nothing else than a turning away from good; for they who are in evil spurn good, that is, spiritual good, which is of charity and faith."

From Whence is Evil?

Swedenborg's most complete answer to this essential question of theodicy is found in the work *Conjugial Love* (or *Marriage Love*). It is placed in parabolic form as a dialogue between Swedenborg and two angels, who, having died as young children, were raised in heaven and knew nothing of evil. In *Conjugial Love* 444, Swedenborg has an exchange with the angels:

"Do you not know that there is such a thing as good and evil, and that good exists from creation, but not evil? And yet evil regarded in itself is not nothing, even though it is nothing good?

"Good exists from creation, and good moreover in the highest degree and in the least degree; and when this least good reduces to nothing, evil arises on the other side. Therefore there is no proportional relationship or progression of good to evil, but a proportional relationship and progression of good to a greater or lesser good, and of evil to a greater or lesser evil; for good and evil are opposites in every single respect.

"Now because good and evil are opposites, there is a middle ground, and in it an area of equilibrium, in which evil acts against good. But because evil does not prevail, it remains in the endeavor. Every person grows up in this equilibrium; and being an equilibrium between good and evil, or to say the same thing, between heaven and hell, it is a spiritual equilibrium, which produces a state of freedom in those who live in it. The Lord draws all people out of this equilibrium to him, and the person who follows in freedom is led by him out of evil into good, and thus into heaven. . . ."

"How could evil come into existence when nothing but good existed from creation? For anything to exist it must have an origin. Good could not be the origin of evil, because evil is nothing good, being rather the negation and destruction of good. But still, because evil exists and is experienced, it is not nothing, but something. Tell us, therefore, from what this something, after having no existence, came into existence."

To that I replied, "This secret cannot be explained unless it is known that no one is good but God alone [cf. Mt. 19:17], and that nothing is good that is good in itself unless it is from God. Consequently it is the person who looks to God and wills to be led by God who is motivated by good. But the person who turns away from God and wills to be led by himself is not motivated by good; for the good that he does is either for the sake of himself or for the sake of the world; thus it is either merit-seeking, or feigned, or hypocritical. From this it is apparent that man himself is the origin of evil—not that that origin was infused into man from creation, but that by turning from God to self he infused it into himself.

"This origin of evil did not exist in Adam and his wife until the serpent said, '. . . in the day you eat of (the tree of the knowledge of good and evil)...you will be like God' (Genesis 3:5). And then, because they turned away from God, and turned to themselves as though to a god, they created in themselves the origin of evil. Eating of that tree symbolized their believing that a person knows good and evil and is wise on his own, and not from God."

But then the two angels asked, "How could man turn away from God and turn to himself, when a person can will nothing, think nothing, and so do nothing except from God. Why did God permit it?"

However, I replied, "Man was so created that everything he wills, thinks and does appears to him as being in him and thus from him. Without this appearance a person would not be a human being, for he would be unable to receive anything of good and truth or of love and wisdom, retain it, and seemingly adopt it as his own. Consequently it follows that without this, as it were, living appearance, man would not have any conjunction with God, and so neither any eternal life. But if as a result of this appearance he persuades himself to the belief that he wills, thinks, and thus does good of himself, and not from the Lord (even though to all appearance as though of himself), he turns good into evil in him, and so creates in him the origin of evil. This was Adam's sin.

"But let me explain this matter a little more clearly: . . . A person who looks with his face to the Lord receives wisdom from him, and through that wisdom, love. But a person who looks away from the Lord receives love and not wisdom; and love without wisdom is love that originates with man and not from the Lord. Moreover, because this love allies itself with falsities, it does not acknowledge God, but embraces itself as a god; and this it tacitly defends by the person's faculty of understanding and of becoming wise as though of himself, implanted in him from creation. Thus this love is the origin of evil."

Using the teachings in this passage as a general outline of Swedenborg's perspective on the origin of evil, let us look in more detail at some of the ideas that are presented.

Any intimation that God can be the source of evil in any way is absolutely rejected. God created man in His image and likeness, and our life is solely from God: "We are because God is," he writes in *Divine Providence* 46. But what we do with our life is up to us; it is a function of our own free choice, and we cannot blame God for our evils. An answer is found in *True Christian Religion*, section 490:

> Unless freedom of choice in spiritual things had been given to man, not man, but God himself, would have been the cause of evil, and thus God would have been the creator both of good and of evil. But to think that God created evil is abominable. Because God gave man freedom of choice in spiritual things he did not create evil, neither does He ever inspire any evil into man, for the reason that he is good itself, and in that good is omnipresent, continually urging and importuning to be received; and even when not received, He does not withdraw; for if he were to withdraw, man would instantly die, nay, would lapse into non-entity; for man's life, and the subsistence of all things of which he consists, are from God. God did not create evil, but evil was introduced by man himself, since man turns the good which is continually flowing in from God into evil, whereby he turns himself away from God and toward himself.

But could God have prevented the existence of evil by not endowing man with free will? Again, *True Christian Religion*, section 489:

It may be thought that giving to man freedom of choice in spiritual things was the mediate cause of evil; consequently, that if such freedom of choice had not been given him, he could not have transgressed. But, my friend, pause here, and consider whether anyone could have been so created as to be human without freedom of choice in spiritual things. If deprived of that, he would be no longer a human being but only a statue. What is freedom of choice but the power to will and do, and to think and speak to all appearance as if of oneself? Because this power was given to man in order that he might live as a man, two trees were placed in the garden of Eden, the tree of life and the tree of the knowledge of good and evil; and this signifies that because of the freedom given him, man is able to eat of the fruit of the tree of life or of the fruit of the tree of knowledge of good and evil.

When Swedenborg speaks in this passage of the Garden of Eden and man's "transgression," it should not be thought that he endorses the idea of "original sin" in the sense that this term is accepted in the Christian tradition. He does acknowledge, however, that there is in every person an inborn heredity of evil—a kind of universal karma (although he does not use this term)—that can either be confirmed or rejected by the individual.

If we are born with this burden of inherited evil, for which we are not responsible, are we, then, inevitably condemned to hell because of it? Such an idea could certainly not be reconciled with a merciful and loving God. What is the nature of this inheritance, and what effect does it have on us?

Man is not born into actual evils, but only into an *inclination* to evils, but with a greater, or less proclivity towards particular evils; consequently, after death man is not judged from any inherited evil, but from the actual evils which he himself has committed.

True Christian Religion 521

[Hereditary evil] is believed to consist in doing evil; but it consists in willing and hence thinking evil; hereditary evil being in the will itself and in the thought thence derived; and being the very *conatus* or endeavor that is therein, and which adjoins itself even when the man is doing what is good. It is known by the delight that is felt when evil befalls another. This root lies deeply hidden, for the very inward form that receives from heaven (that is, through heaven from the Lord) what is good and true, is depraved, and so to speak, distorted; so that when goodness and truth flow in from the Lord, they are either reflected, or perverted, or suffocated. . . . It is from hereditary evil to love self more than others, to will evil to others if they do not honor us, to perceive delight in revenge, and also to love the world more than heaven; and from the same source come all the derivative cupidities or evil affections.

Arcana Coelestia 4317:5

[Hereditary evil] does not manifest itself until a person becomes an adult and acts from his understanding and the derivative will, and meanwhile it lies hidden, especially during infancy. In the Lord's mercy, no one is blamed for what is hereditary, but for what is

actual, and what is hereditary cannot become actual until the
person acts from his own understanding and his own will.

Arcana Coelestia 4563:2

The last sentence in this series of passages is extremely important within the framework of Swedenborg's theology. Once an
individual has reached the age and intellectual development when
he can make rational decisions, he or she bears personal responsibility for his choices. But for evil actually to become one's own, to
become part of a person's spiritual character, it must be confirmed
in both the understanding and the will. This means that we must
know rationally that something is evil and then desire to do it,
even if we do not act on our desire because we are afraid of the
consequences of our action. Evil thoughts by themselves, when
not enjoyed and indulged in, or evil desires that are not justified
intellectually, and thus not made permissible, do not become part
of us. He explains in *Divine Providence* 81:

> The evils which a person believes to be allowable, even though he
> does not commit them, are also appropriated to him; since what-
> ever is allowable in the thought comes from the will, for then there
> is consent. When, therefore, a person believes any evil to be
> allowable, he loosens an internal restraint upon it, and he is
> withheld from doing it only by external restraints, such as fears;
> and because his spirit favors that evil, when external restraints are
> removed he does it as allowable; and meanwhile, he continually
> does it in his spirit.

In this passage, we have an excellent explanation of the spiritual state that Jesus speaks about in the Sermon on the Mount, for example, when he says: "You have heard that it was said to those of old, 'You shall not commit adultery.' But I say to you that whoever looks at a woman to lust for her has already committed adultery with her in his heart" (Matthew 5:27–28).

Where did evil came from in the first place? Swedenborg declares that "evils . . . did not exist until after creation" (*Canons.* "God" vi:10). Evil became possible only after humankind fell away from its primordial connection with the Divine by perverting the human selfhood that was transparent to its Creator, so that it degenerated into ego, which resulted in the illusion that we live from ourselves, rather than from God. Most religious traditions include a belief in some sort of "Golden Age" (Swedenborg calls it the "Most Ancient Church"), in which humanity existed in complete harmony with both the physical and spiritual worlds; a period when the order, unity, and beauty of the macrocosm was reflected without distortion in the finite microcosm. As Swedenborg expresses it in his *Spiritual Diary* 4607:

> Man was created after the entire image of the macrocosm—after the image of heaven, and after the image of the world. His internal is after the image of heaven, his external after the image of the world. Wherefore, it was thus provided, by the Divine, that the Divine may pass over, by means of man, from the spiritual world into the natural world, and be terminated in the ultimate of nature, to wit, in the corporeal (of man), and thus, through man, there should be

connection of the spiritual world with the natural world; so that, by means of man, universal nature may glorify the Lord the Creator.

During this primeval era, hell did not yet exist. In Swedenborg's theology, the inceptions of hell and evil were simultaneous, and hell and evil are synonymous: "Evil in man is hell in him, for it is the same thing whether you say evil or hell. And since man is the cause of his own evil he is led into hell, not by the Lord but by himself" (*Heaven and Hell* 547).

A central doctrine in Swedenborg's theological writings is that every human being is created to be a receptacle, a vessel that may choose to receive and assimilate either goodness or evil. In order that we may have free will, God permits us to feel as though our life is our own, even though it is only "in Him [that] we live and move and have our being." The two divine gifts of freedom and rationality are intrinsic to humanity and are the means whereby our choices are made. According to Swedenborg, there is a continual influx into the human mind from both heaven and hell, and each person is free to accept one or the other, and make it his own. There is a spiritual law that may be expressed as "influx is according to the state of the receiving vessel." The Sufis, too, say that "the color of the water is the color of the bowl that contains it." What we choose to receive as goodness and truth, and what we therefore love, are in accordance with the nature, character, and form of our spirit:

> The truth is that the life of everyone—of mortal, of spirit, and also of angel—flows in solely from the Lord, who is life itself; and

diffuses itself through the whole heaven and also through hell, thus into everyone . . . but the life which flows in is received by each one according to his disposition. Goodness and truth are received as goodness and truth by the good; but goodness and truth are received as evil and falsity by the evil, and are also turned into evil and falsity in them. The case with this is comparatively like the light of the sun, which diffuses itself into all the objects of the earth, but is received according to the quality of each object, and becomes of a beautiful color in beautiful forms, and of a disagreeable color in disagreeable forms.

Arcana Coelestia 2888

In reading Swedenborg's works, it is possible to see a dualist tenor in his theology, embodied in terms of heaven and hell, good and evil spirits, angels and demons. On a deeper level, though, what is expressed in these metaphors is actually a moral dualism of the Zoroastrian type, where heaven and hell are within the individual as states of mind. Swedenborg writes, for example, in *Divine Providence* 93 that "the delight of evil when perceived as good is hell." These states are externalized in postmortem spiritual existence as "appearances," that is, a person's affections—for good or evil—are projected outside of himself as seemingly tangible realities that correspond to and reflect his own internal world—a world of beauty or a world of ugliness—since "The person who is in evil, and thence in falsity, is a microcosm of hell; and the person who is in good, and thence in truth, is a microcosm of heaven" (*Arcana Coelestia* 5339):

Hell and heaven are near to man, indeed, in man—hell in an evil person, and heaven in a good person. Everyone comes after death into that hell or into that heaven in which he has been while in the world. But the state is then changed: the hell which was not perceived in the world becomes perceptible, and the heaven which was not perceived in the world becomes perceptible, the heaven full of all happiness, and the hell of all unhappiness.

Arcana Coelestia 8918

The externalization of these interior states is reminiscent of certain teachings in the *Bardo Thödol*, the "Tibetan Book of the Dead," where the individual who is dying on the physical plane of existence is instructed about the appearances of the spiritual world: "These realms are not come from somewhere outside [thyself]. They come from within . . . thy heart."[15] And the person is told to repeat, "May I recognize whatever [visions] appear, as the reflections of mine own consciousness."[16]

In Swedenborg's theology, there is no single personification of evil in the form of Satan or some other archdevil. The macrocosm in the integrity of its perfection is said to be in the human form. Swedenborg uses the term "form" in a manner that is quite distinct from "shape": form relates to what is spiritual, shape to what is physical. Form is the organization of spiritual qualities, such as love and wisdom, goodness and truth, affection and thought. In this sense, the form of the Lord's kingdom is the *Maximus Homo*, the "Great Human": "The angelic heaven before the Lord is as one Human, whose soul and life is the Lord" (*Divine Providence* 254).

This concept is similar to that of Purusha in Hinduism, Adam Qadmon, or Adam 'Elah in the Jewish mystical tradition of the Kabbalah, and Insān al-Kāmil in Islam. In Swedenborg's works, however, the image of hell is also represented in a form, but one that is the antithesis of the beautiful human form of heaven: "Hell also is in the human form; but it is in a monstrous human form" (*Divine Providence* 204); "The universal hell represents one monstrous devil" (*True Christian Religion* 32:6). Swedenborg often uses the expression "of the devil and from the devil," as when he says: "Evils ought to be shunned, because they are of the devil, and from the devil" (*Brief Exposition* 43). This may be seen as an accommodation to the understanding of those in the Christian tradition, for whom the phrase is quite familiar. For Swedenborg, though, "evil," "hell," and "the devil" are synonymous: "It is the same thing whether you say evil or hell" (*Heaven and Hell* 547); "All evil and falsity are from hell, that is, from the devil, for hell is the devil" (*Arcana Coelestia* 4151).

Why Does God Permit Evil?

The question of why God permits evil to exist in His creation is one that is answered in considerable detail in Swedenborg's theological writings. Swedenborg posits several modalities in the Divine operation, as we see in *Arcana Coelestia* 9940:

> The things which are from the Lord are either nearer to, or more remote from Him; and they are said to be "from His will," "from

good pleasure," "from leave," and "from permission." The things which are from will are most nearly from Him; those which are from good pleasure are somewhat more remotely from Him; those which are from leave still more remotely; and those which are from permission are most remotely from Him.

The word *remote* in this passage must obviously be thought of in purely spiritual terms, neither spatially nor temporally, since God, as infinite and eternal, is beyond time and space.

"Permission" is intimately connected with the free will that God has given to the human being, and Swedenborg defines it in those terms: "To leave man from his freedom to do evil also, is called permission" (*Arcana Coelestia* 10778). "If a person were not permitted to think in accordance with the delights of his life's love, he would no longer be human, for he would lose his two faculties called liberty and rationality, in which humanity itself consists" (*Divine Providence* 281).

It is according to the Divine Providence that everyone is allowed to act from freedom in accordance with reason . . . ; and without permissions man cannot be led from evil by the Lord, and consequently cannot be reformed and saved. For unless evils were allowed to break out, man would not see them and therefore would not acknowledge them, and thus could not be induced to resist them. Hence it is that evils cannot be repressed by any act of Providence; for if they were they would remain shut in, and like a disease, such as cancer and gangrene, they would spread and consume everything vital in man.

No one can be withdrawn from his hell by the Lord unless he sees that he is in hell and wishes to be led out; and this cannot be done without permissions, the causes of which are laws of the Divine Providence.

Divine Providence 251

As is indicated by this passage, the permission of evil is to be thought of as within the context of God's infinite and eternal Divine Providence, which "regards eternal things, and not temporal things except so far as they accord with eternal things" (*Divine Providence* 249)—specifically, the ultimate salvation of as many people as possible.

Swedenborg makes a very interesting distinction between divine providence and divine foresight. It is worth quoting several passages from his works that discuss this subject, since the attribute of God's omniscience—of which both providence and foresight are elements in Swedenborg's theology—has been often used as an argument against free will and in favor of predestination.

It is an undoubtable fact that the Lord governs the universe. This government is called Providence. But since evils, likewise permissions, are not provided but foreseen, in order to understand this (it must be known) that foresight relates to evils; Providence is the disposal of them to good ends. Nevertheless, there is no such thing as chance, that is, no evil happens by chance, but all evils are so governed that not one of them is permitted which is not conducive to good, both to man and soul. Moreover, nothing is permitted which has not thus been foreseen, for otherwise it could by no means happen; consequently, the various evils are so turned that certain ones, and not others occur, because it cannot be otherwise in a state so perverse. Thus it is Providence alone which governs, for foresight is thus turned into Providence, and in this way those evils are provided from which there may be good.

Spiritual Diary 1088

Providence is predicated of good, but foresight of evil; for all good flows in from the Lord, and therefore this is provided; but all evil is from hell, or from man's ego which makes one with hell; and therefore this is foreseen. As regards evil, Providence is nothing but the direction or determination of evil to less evil, and as far as possible to good; but the evil itself is foreseen.

Arcana Coelestia 5155

As regards foresight and providence in general, it is foresight relatively to man, and providence relatively to the Lord. The Lord foresaw from eternity what the human race would be, and what would be the quality of each member of it, and that evil would continually increase, until at last man of himself would rush headlong into hell. On this account the Lord has not only provided means by which man may be turned from hell and led to heaven, but also from providence He continually turns and leads him. The Lord also foresaw that it would be impossible for any good to be rooted in man except in his freedom, for whatever is not rooted in freedom is dissipated on the first approach of evil and temptation. This the Lord foresaw, and also that man of himself, or from his freedom, would incline toward the deepest hell; and therefore the Lord provides that if a man should not suffer himself to be led in freedom to heaven, he may still be bent toward a milder hell; but that if he should suffer himself to be led in freedom to good, he may be led to heaven. This shows what foresight means, and what providence, and that what is foreseen is thus provided. And from this we can see how greatly the person errs who believes that the Lord has not foreseen, and does not see, the veriest singulars appertaining to man, and that in these He does not foresee and lead; when the truth is that the Lord's foresight and providence are in the very minutest of these veriest singulars connected with man, in things so very minute that it is impossible by any thought to comprehend as much as one out of a hundred millions of them; for every smallest moment of man's life involves a series of consequences extending to eternity, each moment being as a new beginning to those which follow; and so with all and each of the moments of his life, both of his understanding and of his will.

Arcana Coelestia 3854:2–3

As can, hopefully, be seen from this summary of Swedenborg's theodicy, his approach resolves many of the problems that are evident in earlier attempts at dealing with the issue of evil. In his theological writings, Swedenborg presents clearly, systematically, and consistently the teachings of the *religio perennis*—the divine truth that has been revealed to humanity from time immemorial.

In Swedenborg's works, however, that truth is presented without the parochial and sectarian accretions that are found in the exoteric doctrines of individual religious traditions. Swedenborg often acknowledges the transcendent unity that constitutes the essence of all religions, and in one of his visionary states, he reports: "I have heard that churches [i.e., religions] which are in different varieties of goodness and truth, provided their goodness relates to love to the Lord, and their truths to faith in Him, are like so many gems in a king's crown" (*True Christian Religion* 763). He also says that "the heavenly Human [form], which is heaven . . . cannot be composed of people all of one religion but of people of many religions" (*Divine Providence* 326). For Swedenborg, the variety of religious expression among the peoples of the earth are a reflection of the unity in variety that characterizes heaven.

Swedenborg's message is one of great hope for all humanity. He says: "This vast system which is called the universe is a work coherent as a unit from things first to things last, because in creating it God had a single end in view, which was an angelic heaven from the human race; and all things of which the world consists are means to that end" (*True Christian Religion* 13). It is up to each individual to cooperate with God in the realization of that end, and cooperation means being aware of the evils into which we are led by our ego, and consciously rejecting them, since there is a universal spiritual law that, of necessity, has two poles: "Everyone is born for heaven, and no one for hell; and from the Lord each comes into heaven, and into hell from self" (*Conjugial Love* 350).

In order to follow the path that leads to a heavenly state, it is necessary for us to reflect not only on our acts, but especially on our motivations. What do we think about when we are alone? In what directions do our thoughts lead us? What would we do if we were not restrained by fear of civil laws or the loss of our reputation? These are questions that Swedenborg says we must ask ourselves—not to the point of obsessiveness, since that would involve a preoccupation with ourselves, a trap of the ego that is to be avoided, but in general, so that it becomes a matter of almost unconscious practice.

Swedenborg continually reminds us that our most cherished belief—that we live solely from ourselves—is our most fundamental fallacy, and that in order to attain to the happiness God intends for us, we need to acknowledge wholeheartedly that it is a fallacy, and joyfully accept the fact that we live from God alone, so that his will may become our will in all that we love, and think, and say, and do:

> If any individual had a grain of will and intelligence of his own that "one" could not possibly exist, but would be rent asunder; and with it would perish that Divine Form which can only manifest itself and continue in being when the Lord is the All in all people and they are absolutely nothing. To think and to will from self is the essential Divine principle, while to think and to will from God is the essential human principle; and what is essentially Divine cannot be appropriated to any man, for in that case man would be God.
>
> Keep this in mind; and if you wish, you will have it confirmed by angels when after death you enter into the spiritual world.

Divine Providence 293

Notes

1. Archibald MacLeish, *J.B. A Play in Verse* (Boston: Houghton Mifflin Company, 1956), 14. Reprinted by permission of Houghton Mifflin Company.

2. Lactantius, *A Treatise on the Anger of God*, translated by William Fletcher, in Alexander Roberts and James Donaldson, eds., *Ante-Nicene Fathers*, vol. 7 (1886; reprint, Peabody, Massachusetts: Hendrickson Publishers, Inc., 1994), 271.

3. A. V. Williams Jackson, *Zoroastrian Studies* (1928; reprint, New York: AMS Press, 1965), 205.

4. Eugen Drewermann, *Strukturen des Bösen*, I: *Die jahwistische Urgeschichte in exegetischer Sicht* (Paderborn, Schöningh, 1995), 106 ff.

5. Herbert Haag, *Vor dem Bösen ratlos?* (Munich: Piper Verlag, 1978), 23.

6. Rudolf Bultmann, *Theology of the New Testament* (London: SCM Press, 1965), vol. 2, 21.

7. *Manichäische Handschriften der Staatlichen Museen Berlin*, Bd. 1: *Kephalaia* (Stuttgart: W. Kohlhammer Verlag, 1940), 220.

8. For a full treatment of Augustine's views on this subject, see his *De libero arbitrio* (On Free Will).

9. Pseudo-Dionysius, *Complete Works*, translated by Colm Luibheid (New York: Paulist Press, 1987), 85.

10. Ibid., 85.

11. Ibid., 86.

12. Ibid., 85–86.

13. Ibid., 91.

14. John Hick, *Evil and the Love of God*, second edition (1966; San Francisco: Harper, 1977), 385.

15. W. Y. Evans-Wentz, comp. and ed., *The Tibetan Book of the Dead*, third edition (Oxford: Oxford University Press, 1957), 121.

16. Ibid., 103.

Debates
with Devils

I

Swedenborg and the Devil

"Mark you this, Bassanio, the devil can cite Scripture for his purpose." This Shakespearean line bespeaks the intriguing fact that, when the devil in the wilderness addressed Jesus, even he quoted Scripture in his words of temptation. According to the Bible, Jesus did not usually allow the devils to speak. (See, for example Luke 4:41.) But there are cases in which they do speak, and their words become part of the gospel record. The first chapter of Mark describes what happened when Jesus proclaimed a powerful message. Evil spirits couldn't bear it. "Let us alone! What have we to do with you?" they protested. On a later occasion, Jesus asked a spirit to declare his name; who can forget that reply? "My name is Legion; for we are many."

Words conniving evil spirits might speak make up one of the classics of religious literature, namely, *The Screwtape Letters* by

3

C. S. Lewis. The devilish dialogue is contrived by Lewis, and his book is a piece of fiction, but something continues to ring true in that work for millions of readers. The perspective it puts on human life makes us more thoughtful, more aware, and stronger in efforts to live wisely with good will towards others.

All the words of evil spirits in the book you will soon read were reported by Emanuel Swedenborg. The question has often been asked whether or not Swedenborg merely imagined he heard such things. I prefer to leave the answer to this question to the reader, but whether they were heard from another world (as Swedenborg claims) or were merely imagined or invented, they are presented with the hope that they will provide a perspective on the human condition.

Scattered in the theological volumes penned by Swedenborg are encounters in which devils express their point of view. In some instances, they may be disagreeing with angels. In others, Swedenborg himself converses with them; on occasion, he banters with them when they voice their challenges. Two examples of this are easy to find, because they occur at the very end of two of Swedenborg's better known books.

At the end of *Divine Providence,* devils complain that only the views of angels have been expressed. They want something said from their viewpoint. Swedenborg asks them what they want him to say for them. They want it known that devils have their delights too. Swedenborg quizzes them about those delights and finds out that they are pathetic and disgusting. Then, at the end of *True Christian Religion,* devils challenge Swedenborg to perform miracles to validate his claims. Swedenborg banters with them about the effect of miracles on rational thought.

While these two examples are easily located at the end of major volumes, most of the material of this kind is, as already mentioned, scattered in several long books. We have collected many of them so that they may be presented in fresh English translation. They are grouped at the end of each chapter.

Swedenborg's Mission

Swedenborg believed there was a purpose in his encounters with evil spirits. He did not regard his ability to speak with them as something achieved by himself. He said it was *granted* to him. "It has been granted me to associate with angels and to talk with them person to person, also to see what is in the heavens and what is in the hells." In *Arcana Coelestia* 7479, for example, he writes:

> I spoke with some spirits . . . They were amazed at the presence of so many evil spirits around me and at the fact that these would also talk to me. But I was given to answer that they were allowed to do so in order that I might learn what they were like and the reason they were in hell, which has to do with the way they lived.[1]

The reader may wonder whether Swedenborg always believed in angels and spirits and how his understanding of them evolved

---

1. As is customary in Swedenborgian studies, the numbers following titles of Swedenborg's works refer to paragraph or section numbers, which are uniform in all editions, rather than to page numbers.

as he entered into his mission. The religious belief in which he was reared included a belief in spirits both benign and malignant. To the typical Lutheran clergyman of Swedenborg's time, Satan was a real person to be reckoned with. Certainly, Swedenborg's father, Jesper, a Lutheran bishop, believed this to be true.

While Swedenborg does mention "Satan" or the "Evil One" in the years prior to the time when he claimed to be allowed to see the realities of heaven and hell, in his theological teachings, while maintaining the symbolic use of the term "the devil," he says that there is not one evil individual or being in charge of hell. Indeed, he states God is in charge of all realms![2] For Swedenborg the terms "devil" and "Satan" are useful to depict the whole of hell in aggregate or the force of evil in general. In his theology, Swedenborg will say that evils are to be shunned because they are "of the devil and from the devil," but he is using the term in a symbolic way. Actually, when he talks of a "devil," a "satan," or an "evil spirit," he is talking about beings who have chosen to turn away from God. The following quotation from *Arcana Coelestia* 968 shows what Swedenborg means when he speaks of "the devil."

> [After numerous experiences], I finally had no fear whatever of talking to even the worst of hell's mob. And that is exactly what I was allowed to do, in order to learn what they were like.
>
> To those who were surprised that I talked with such spirits, I was given to say further, "The experience did me no harm; but more

---

2. See *Heaven and Hell*. The first chapter that deals with hell (chapter 56) is entitled "The Lord Rules the Hells."

than this, you have to remember that those who are devils in the next life were once mortal human beings—the ones who carried on a life filled with hatred, revenge, and adultery when they were in the world. Some of them had a better reputation than other people. In fact, certain ones of them were acquaintances of mine while they still lived in their bodies. The term 'devil' only means a crowd of people like this in hell.

"Besides, while people are still living in their bodies, they have at least two spirits from hell with them, in addition to two angels from heaven. With evil people, the angels regulate the hellish spirits, but with good people the hellish spirits are subdued and forced to be of service.

"As a result, it's misguided to think that any devil has existed since the beginning of creation other than those who were once mortals of this type."

They were dumbfounded to hear this, and admitted that they had held a completely different opinion concerning the devil and the devil's crew.

Can We Actually Believe in Devils?

Of course, allusions to devils appear again and again in the literature of the world, among them Christopher Marlow and the German writer Goethe, who both wrote of Faust's selling his soul to a particular devil named Mephistopheles. (According to medieval legend, Mephistopheles was one of seven chief devils.) There are memorable lines in English literature on the devil theme.

William Cowper, who wrote in the late 1700s, penned the lines, "And Satan trembles, when he sees/The weakest saint upon his knees."

Shakespeare's writings are an eminent example of the English literature that was well known to continental Europeans of Swedenborg's time. Sometimes devils are as figments of imagination in which "one sees more devils than vast hell can hold" (Midsummer Night's Dream). Shakespeare's accounts resonate with human psychology. "What can the devil speak true?" asks Shakespeare in Macbeth, and then he says, "And oftentimes, to win us to our harm, the instruments of darkness tell us truths, win us with honest trifles, to betray's in deepest consequence." How our minds can be tricked! In Trolius and Cressida Shakespeare observes, "Sometimes we are devils to ourselves when we will tempt the frailty of our powers."

For most writers who mention devils, the Bible is the basic source. This was definitely true of Swedenborg, most of whose written volumes are either Bible exposition or are filled with biblical quotations. As we look at the Bible's portrayal of devils, let us begin with the basic concept of "enemies"—those with which the human mind contends in the watches of the night. Are those enemies merely the ingredients of our own minds? Are they psychological phenomena entirely within ourselves? Or are they in reality entities alien to us?

The Enemies of Our Peace

"You prepare a table before me in the presence of my enemies."
That line is from the best known of all the Psalms, which begins,
"the Lord is my shepherd . . ." Do "enemies" here and elsewhere in
the Psalms refer merely to citizens of some nation that has been
our opponent in war? Are they our social rivals? Are they our
business competitors? They must be more than that.

The assertion we are making is that the enemies of our peace,
the enemies mentioned in Scripture, are the devils or evil spirits in
the unseen world of the spirit. We can look at the Psalms with this
in mind.

Psalm 1 speaks of sinister beings becoming "like chaff which
the wind drives away." Psalm 2 speaks of "the nations" plotting
our destruction. "Let us break their bonds in pieces and cast away
their cords from us" (verse 3). In number 3, the psalmist laments
how multiplied his enemies have become. "Lord, how they have
increased who trouble me! Many are they who say of me, there is
no help for him in God." But the Savior strikes the enemies, and
the psalmist says, "I will not be afraid of ten thousands of people
who have set themselves against me all around."

In the Psalms that follow, the theme recurs like the beating of
waves: "Let them fall by their own counsels." "Let all my enemies
be ashamed and greatly troubled; let them turn back" (6:10). "Save
me from all those who persecute me; and deliver me, lest they tear
me like a lion, rending me in pieces, while there is none to deliver"
(7:1). "When my enemies turn back, they shall fall and perish at
Your presence" (9:3). "Consider my trouble from those who hate

me, You who lift me up from the gates of death. . . . The wicked shall be turned into hell" (9:13, 17).

As we proceed through the Psalms, we read of the voice of the enemy, the oppression of the enemy, and the malice and deception of the enemy. Psalm 110 contains the phrase: "Till I make your enemies your footstool," quoted by Jesus in each of the synoptic gospels. According to Swedenborg, the mission of Jesus was to contend with and subjugate the enemies of our spirits. Swedenborg writes of the spiritual dimension of the human condition, saying we are inhabitants of two worlds. Our bodies are in the natural world, but as to our spirits we have another environment.

While our spiritual environment is, for the most part, beyond our consciousness, there is, as it were, a gateway. One of the Psalms concludes with a reference to the gate: Psalm 127 states, "Unless the Lord guards the city, the watchman stays awake in vain. It is vain for you to rise up early, to sit up late, to eat the bread of sorrows; for so he gives his beloved sleep." Delivered from fear and shame "they shall speak with their enemies in the gate." Secure in sleep, and safe in wakefulness, the hero of the Psalm 127 is prepared to encounter the enemy at the gate.

One is reminded of the story of Jacob who awakened from sleep having seen in a dream the ascent and descent of the angels of God. There was so much more to life than he had imagined. This world is a threshold. He exclaimed, "How awesome is this place! This is none other than the house of God, and this is the gate of heaven" (Genesis 28:17).

As a descendent of Abraham, Jacob was under the promise of

"possessing the gate of the enemy" (Genesis 22:17). Concerning this, Swedenborg writes in *Arcana Coelestia* 2851:2:

> As regards the meaning of "a gate," there are in general two gates with each individual person. One gate is exposed towards hell and is open to evil and falsities from there. In that gate demons and spirits from hell are present. The other gate is exposed towards heaven and is open to goods and truths from there. In that gate angels are present . . . For there are two paths which lead into a person's rational mind, a higher or internal path along which good and truth from the Lord enter in, and a lower or external path along which evil and falsity enter in surreptitiously from hell. In the middle is the rational mind towards which the two paths converge. From the goods and truths present there the rational mind is compared in the Word to a city and is actually called a city. And because it is compared to and actually called a city it is depicted as having gates, and is described in various places as having enemies, that is, evil demons and spirits, besieging it and assaulting it, while angels from the Lord are defending it.

In the first chapter of Luke, we read, "that we should be saved from our enemies and from the hand of all who hate us." Devils from hell may be described as those who hate. Jesus said to his followers that they would be hated (Matt. 10:22). "If the world hates you, you know that it hated me before it hated you" (John 10:18). It can be a good sign if one is hated, for the unseen enemies of our peace hate what is good. "Blessed are you" when they hate you! (Luke 6:22).

What the Bible Says about the Devil

Elsewhere in the Bible, we find both the specific use of "devils" in the plural and a more symbolic personification of evil as a serpent, a dragon, a demon. The Hebrew word *Satan* means an accuser or an adversary. The term is used in the sixth verse of Psalm 109. English-language Bibles generally use the phrase "an accuser," but the King James Version says, "Let Satan stand at his right hand." Both renderings are justifiable.

While there are a host of individual passages in the Hebrew Bible and New Testament portraying the source of evil, it is helpful to step back and consider the general picture. The first book of the Bible presents the image of a serpent, and the last book recalls that image, identifying that serpent as "the Devil and Satan." The third chapter of Genesis begins: "Now the serpent was more cunning that any beast of the field . . . and he said to the woman . . ." Swedenborg's theological view is that this narrative is richly but symbolically filled with truth. Thus, rather than a literal talking snake, the serpent symbolizes the influence of sensual thinking, the thinking that casts doubt on anything that cannot be felt with the senses of the body. This is the voice that says there is no such things as love, that there is no God.

As the Bible begins with the symbolism of the garden of Eden, it concludes with the vivid symbols of Revelation or the Apocalypse. In the twelfth chapter of the Apocalypse, a "sign" appears, a great red dragon whose tail brings down a third of the stars of heaven: "The great dragon was cast out, that serpent of old, called the Devil and Stan, who deceives the whole world."

While from the point of view of Swedenborg's theology there is not one single devil, Swedenborg testifies that the whole of hell may be regarded as one giant monster. In one of Swedenborg's visions, he reports seeing in the distance a serpent offering a piece of fruit, but as he draws near in spirit, he sees "instead of the serpent a monstrosity of a person."

We have mentioned the Hebrew word *Satan*. However, in the Hebrew Scriptures, there are very few references to "devils," and they are plural references, for example the reference to sacrificing to devils (Deuteronomy 32:17, Psalm 106:37). The Hebrew root meaning is "a hairy one" or "a destroyer." It is in the New Testament that the word *devil* comes into use (*daimon* or *diabolos*). In the Gospel of John, we are told that "the devil" put it in the heart of Judas Iscariot to betray Jesus. Luke simply states, "Then Satan entered Judas." In anticipation of this, Jesus said to the twelve disciples, "One of you is a devil" (John 6:70). The casting out of devils was one of the marked features of the ministry of Jesus, who also gave the disciples the power to do so. According to Swedenborg's theology, Jesus was attacked by all the forces of hell, and this we will refer to later in this book. Near the beginning of each of the synoptic gospels, there is an account of Jesus' being tempted in the wilderness after which the devil "departed from him until an opportune time" (Luke 4:13).

The "Lord of the Flies" and "Lucifer"

From the Bible, we can see that the nations of the land of Canaan had their deities and demons and that sometimes the beliefs of surrounding nations affected the faith of the children of Israel. The name Beelzebub is translated "the lord of the flies." Swedenborg notes that, in a number of cases, the deities or demons were men of special influence who were popularly deified by followers after their death. Such was the case with Beelzebub, a god of the Philistines (see Swedenborg's *True Christian Religion* 292). Eventually, this man became equated with Satan (see Swedenborg's *Apocalypse Explained* 740:10).

The reason Jesus was accused of working with Beelzebub was that an occasion arose in which the power of Jesus over demons became undeniable. When Jesus healed the man, he "both spoke and saw" (Matthew 12:22). It was obvious that something great had happened. "The multitudes were amazed," and they began to ask one another whether Jesus was the promised one. "But when the Pharisees heard it they said, 'This fellow does not cast out demons except by Beelzebub, the ruler of the demons.'"

Although the name Beelzebub has since become one of the satanic appellations, a much better known such appellation is Lucifer, a word with an interesting story.

It is no wonder that people think that the Bible talks about "Lucifer," because it does seem to occur in a verse of the Bible. Here is how it happened. In Isaiah 14, there is a speech against the king of Babylon. In that speech, a word occurs which, for centuries, was not associated with the devil nor with the Latin word *lucifer.* The word is *helel* which means a shining one or a day star (Isaiah 14:12). The king of Babylon is chided: "Have you become as weak as we? . . . Your pomp is brought down to hell. . . . You have said in your heart, I will ascend into heaven. I will exalt my throne above the stars of God . . . Yet you shall be brought down to hell."

Hundreds of years passed before the idea was attached to this part of Isaiah that there was an angel of heaven who was expelled. Late in the fourth century CE, the idea was introduced that a saying of Jesus in the New Testament could be linked to the verses in Isaiah about someone's being cast down to hell. The monk and scholar who came up with this was Jerome who lived from 340 to 420 CE. Jerome noted the words in Luke, "I saw Satan fall like lightning from heaven." He linked this with the Isaiah passage about the king of Babylon. But "I saw Satan fall as lightning from heaven" was said about what was taking place during the ministry of Jesus.

The subjugation of the hells was part of the mission of Jesus, who said as the time of the crucifixion drew near, "Now is the judgment of this world. Now shall the prince of this world be cast out" (John 12:31). He had been casting out devils, who infested many people at that time. He gave power to the disciples to do the same, and they came back reporting with joy, "Lord, even the demons are subject to us in your name." Those disciples could not see the demons any more than could the people to whom they ministered; but at this point, Jesus could say that he beheld the falling of Satan from heaven and that he was giving to the disciples authority "over all the power of the enemy." "Nevertheless do not rejoice in this, that the spirits are subject to you, but rather rejoice because your names are written in heaven" (Luke 10:17-20).

Jerome not only linked the incident recorded in Luke with the saying of Isaiah about the king of Babylon, but, when he produced the first common language (Vulgate) translation of the Bible, he also introduced the name "Lucifer" at Isaiah 14:12. Lucifer in Latin means a bearer of light, and the concept thus arose that there had been an angelic bearer of light who was cast down into hell. In a number of cases, English translations of the Bible have retained the Latin *Lucifer*, and very many people have retained the concept of a fallen angel. More recent translations of the Bible, such as the *New International Version* do not make use of the name Lucifer. Still, that name has become part of our cultural heritage, and someone who owns a black cat with piercing eyes might choose a name that seems to have dark connotations, although the word itself means a bearer of light. It is notable that Swedenborg once conversed with a spirit who had convinced himself that he was the biblical Lucifer (see *Conjugial Love* 269:4).

Let us not simply write off the name Lucifer and the notions that go with it as mere biblical misinterpretation. Yes, the literal meaning of Isaiah 14 applies to the king of Babylon who thought to rise to the heights and yet fell to the depths. But think of the symbolic meaning of that text. Babylon is the symbol of selfish love, specifically the love of dominating over others for self-serving reasons. Babylon's king symbolized selfish love, which is what evil is all about and what hell is all about. That dominating love is symbolically "the devil itself," and so there is reason to respect the belief of those who think of a sinister name (like Lucifer) and equate it with the prince of darkness.

Martin Luther's hymn aptly personifies the enemy of salvation in the famous words, "For still our ancient foe doth seek to work us woe, his craft and power are great, and armed with cruel hate, on earth is not his equal." The apostle Peter warned of the ancient foe, "Be sober, be vigilant, because your adversary the devil walks about like a roaring lion, seeking whom he may devour. Resist him, steadfast in the faith, knowing that the same sufferings are experienced by your brotherhood in the world."

Direct Experience with Devils

We come now to Swedenborg's encounters with devils. We will have a first look at some of the examples of Swedenborg's direct experience, and then we will get from documentary evidence the story of how Swedenborg got to the point at which such things were possible. The episodes that are gathered at the end of each chapter have been newly translated by Lisa Hyatt Cooper.

In this encounter, angels, together with Swedenborg, exchange views with a devil on the subject of basic human loves.

I fell to talking with some angels. Eventually we touched on the craving for evil that affects every human being from birth. "In the world I'm living in," said one, "people afflicted with that desire seem foolish to us angels, although to themselves they appear extremely wise.

"In a process intended to release them from their foolishness, they alternate between this stupidity and a rational state (a superficial condition for them). When rational, they recognize and admit to their insanity, but even so they yearn desperately to return from the rational state into their insane condition. They also give themselves over to it as if fleeing something forced and joyless for something free and pleasurable. It is their intense cravings and not clear thinking that yield them profound satisfaction.

"Three universal loves went into the casting of every human being at creation: love for our fellow human beings, which is also a love of being useful—a spiritual love; love of worldly gain, which is also a love of getting rich—a materialistic love; and love for ourselves, which is also a love of controlling others—a love seated in the body. A person is truly human when love for others or for being useful makes the head, love of worldly gain or of getting rich makes the chest and belly, and love of self or of taking control makes the feet and their soles.

"If love of worldly gain makes the head, we aren't human except in a hunchbacked way. If self-love makes the head, though, we stand not on our feet but on the palms of our hands, head down and buttocks on high.

"When love of being useful makes the head and the other two loves form the trunk and feet, respectively, heaven sees a person as having an angel's face, with a beautiful rainbow circling the head. If love of worldly gain or riches makes the head, heaven sees the pallor of a corpse in the face and a jaundiced halo around the head. And if self-love or a love of controlling others makes the head, heaven sees the face as dark and fervid, with a chalk-white halo."

"What do the halos represent?" I asked.

"Intelligence," they answered. "A chalk-white halo above a dark, fervid face represents the situation in which a person has intelligence outside on the surface but insanity down inside. People like this display wisdom while they're in their bodies but madness when they inhabit their spirits. None of us has wisdom in the spirit unless we receive it from the Lord, which happens when he gives us a new birth and recreates us."

The earth split open on the left, and before my eyes, there rose through the gap a devil with a dusky, feverish face and a white halo. "Who are you?" I inquired.

"I am Lucifer, Son of the Dawn," he said. "Because I claimed a likeness to the Most High I was thrown down, as it says of me in Isaiah 14." He was not Lucifer but only believed he was.

"If you were thrown down," I said, "how can you rise back up out of hell?"

"There I'm a devil, but here I'm an angel of light," he answered. "Don't you see my white halo? If you want, you can see how I'm ethical when I'm with ethical people, rational among the rational ones, and spiritual, in fact, among the spiritual. I've even managed to deliver sermons!"

"What is your theme?"

"I preach against swindlers, adulterers—every lover of hell. I've described myself, Lucifer, as a devil no less! I've called curses down on myself and been praised to the skies for doing so. That's how I took on the epithet 'Son of the Dawn.' And to my own amazement, it has never occurred to me during all my time in the pulpit that I wasn't speaking the absolute truth, and properly so.

"I've learned the reason for this, which is that I was functioning at the time on a shallow level, cut off from my inner thoughts and feelings. But although others have shown me this, I still haven't been able to change, because I've set myself up above the Most High and lifted myself in pride against him."

"How have you been able to speak this way when you're a swindler and an adulterer yourself?" I asked.

"I'm one thing on the surface or in body and another as to my inner depths or spirit," he answered. "In body I'm an angel, but in spirit I'm a devil. That's because, as a physical being, I'm governed by my intellect, while, as a spirit, I'm governed by my will. My intellect carries me up but my will carries me down.

"As long as the intellect rules, a white halo covers my head. But when the intellect abdicates entirely to the will and becomes the will's possession—which is our eventual fate—the halo turns black and dissolves. Then I can't rise into this light any longer."

But, suddenly, seeing the angels with me, he became inflamed in face and voice and turned black all the way up to his halo. Through the opening from which he had risen, he fell back down into hell.

What the angels nearby had seen and heard led them to the conclusion that a person's character is determined by the will rather than the understanding, because the will easily draws the understanding onto its side and dominates it.

"Where do devils get their rational ability?" I then asked the angels.

"It comes from the pride involved in love of self," they said, "A sense of pride envelopes self-love, being the glow cast by that love's burning flame, and it carries the intellect up almost into heaven's light.

"Whenever people know and recognize truth, their intellect is capable of rising to the height of that knowledge. The will cannot rise to the same level unless the person lives a life in keeping with the truth taught by the church and by sound reason.

"This is why the rational faculty in atheists—atheists who take an egotistical pride in their fame and who consequently glory in their own intelligence—is more refined than in many others. But this superiority shows itself only when they're involved in intellectual thought, not when under the sway of the will's love. And the will's love takes hold of the inner self, intellectual thought of the outer."

An angel went on to tell why humans are made of three loves

put together—the love of being useful, the love of worldly gain, and the love of self. "The purpose is to allow us to receive our thoughts from God, even though we seem to be thinking entirely on our own. The highest parts of the human mind turn upward to God, the middle parts aim outward to the world, and the bottom-most parts look down into the body. Since the lowest parts look downward, people are under the full impression that they think on their own, even though the thoughts originate in God."

True Christian Religion 507

Swedenborg wished he could meet people in such material delusion that they want to own all the wealth there is. Together with angels, he descended into hell to do just that.

[Once, in discussing passions, fantasy, and intelligence with a couple of angels,] I asked whether everyone obsessed by a passion is deluded by a fantasy related to it. They answered that the ones who are so deluded are those whose thoughts turn inward, who indulge their imagination too much and end up talking to themselves. This is because they virtually cut their spirit off from its connection with the body, overwhelm their brains with phantasms, and revel in the pretense that they own everything.

Into such madness comes a person after death if he or she has detached spirit from body and refused to give up the pleasure of being mad. Such a person has, to some extent, thought from religion about evil and falsity but not about unrestrained love of self and the way it destroys love of the Lord, or about unrestrained love of worldly goods and the way it destroys love for the neighbor.

The two angels and I found ourselves wanting to see the people who, because of their materialism, had the delusional wish or hallucination of being the owners of all existing wealth; and we perceived that our desire to observe these people was inspired in us in order that we might come to understand them.

Their residences were below the ground we stood on but above hell. Glancing at each other, we agreed to go down. An opening appeared and in it a stairway, which we descended. (The approach, we learned, had to be made from the east. Otherwise, we would enter into the fog of their hallucination, allowing our minds and at the same time our eyes to be clouded over.)

There it was: a house of made of reeds—porous, and standing in a fog that poured steadily out of the house like smoke through the cracks in three walls. On entering, we saw fifty people on one side and fifty on another sitting on benches, their backs turned to the east and south, their faces to the west and north.

In front of each was a table, on the table a number of bulging moneybags, and around the bags a wealth of gold coins. "Are these the riches of everyone in the world?" we asked.

"Not everyone in the world," they said. "Everyone in this country." Their words had a hissing sound. The people themselves had round faces, luminescent as snail shell. The pupils of their eyes, set in green, flashed like lightning—a gleam produced by their fantasies.

"So you think," we said, standing in their midst, "that you own the riches of the whole country."

"We do own them," they said.

"Which one of you?"

"Each of us."

"How can that be? There are lots of you!"

"Each of us knows, 'Anything that person has is mine.' No one is allowed to think, much less to say, 'What's mine is not yours,' but it *is* acceptable to think and say, 'What's yours is mine.'"

The coins on the tables looked like solid gold, even to our eyes. But when we let in light from the east, they turned out to be mere specks of gold that the people magnified this way by joining together in a single grand fantasy. They said that everyone coming in has to bring some gold, which they cut into smaller and smaller pieces. By the strength of their combined fantasy, they then enlarge the fragments into coins of more imposing appearance.

"Weren't you born rational?" we asked. "Where did you come up with this fanciful nonsense?"

"We know it's all empty make-believe," they said. "But because it thrills the deepest reaches of our minds, we come and indulge in the pretense of unlimited ownership. We don't stay more than a few hours, though, before we leave. Each time, we return to our right minds.

"Still, the allure of our fantasies takes over from time to time and forces us to come and go. So by turns we're in and out of our right minds.

"We're also aware that a hard fate awaits anyone who cheats others out of their goods."

"What fate is that?" we asked.

"They're swallowed up," they said, "and forced naked into a prison in hell, where they're kept working for clothes and food. Later they're paid a few pennies, which they collect and pour all the joy of their hearts into. But if they do something bad to their fellow inmates, they have to hand over a portion of their hoard as a fine."

Marriage Love 267; part of 268

Do animals have rational thought? Swedenborg enters into a passionate debate about this question.

Once when I woke from sleep in the half-light of dawn, I seemed to see specters of various shapes before my eyes. Later, when full morning arrived, I saw phantom lights in different forms. Some appeared to be pages full of writing. These were folded over and over until they looked like shooting stars, and they vanished as they fell through the air. Some appeared to be open books, and they either gleamed like small moons or burned like candles. Among them were books that floated up high, where they disintegrated, and books that fell to the ground, where they dissolved into dust.

From these visions, I divined that underneath the meteors were standing people who argued about nonexistent things that they considered tremendously important. In the spiritual world, phenomena like this come into view in the skies from the superficial reasoning of those standing below.

Soon, my spiritual sight opened up to me, and I noticed a number of spirits wearing laurel wreaths around their heads and flowered robes on their bodies, a sign that they were spirits who, in the world, had been famous experts in the natural sciences.

As I was in the spirit, I approached and made my way into the knot of people. There I could hear that they were disagreeing sharply and passionately about intuitive ideas—whether these are present from birth in people, as they are in animals. Those who denied the proposition turned their backs on those who supported it. In the end, the groups stood divided from each other, like the battalions of two separate armies about to join swords in battle. But because they had no swords, they fought with pointed words.

Then, suddenly, a certain angelic spirit stood among them, raised his voice, and said "I was not far from you when I heard you quarreling heatedly on both sides about native intuition. You were disagreeing on whether people have any, as animals do.

"*I'm* telling you, though, that *people aren't born with any ideas and neither are animals.* So you're making a big to-do over nothing. It's horsefeathers, as they say, or the beard on a modern man."[3]

They all flared up at this. "Throw him out!" they roared. "He's defying common sense!"

But when they tried to get rid of him, they saw around him a ring of heavenly light, which they could not breach. He was, after all, an angelic spirit. So they fell back and moved away from him a little.

"Why are you so angry?" he asked them after the halo had been withdrawn. "Listen to me first and mull over the line of reasoning that I offer. Draw a conclusion from it yourselves, and I predict that anyone with sound judgment will yield. This will calm the storms that have brewed in your minds."

"All right," they answered, although grumbling. "Talk and we'll listen."

---

3. Modern men being clean-shaven in 1770, when Swedenborg was writing, the image stands for something that is impossible, as does "horsefeathers" (literally, "[lamb's] wool from a goat").

Then he took up his argument. "You believe that animals have intuitive ideas," he said. "What led you to that conclusion was the fact that their actions appear to be thought out. The truth is that not a whit of thinking is present in animals, and you cannot have ideas without thought.

"The hallmark of thinking is to do such-and-such for this reason or that. Consider, then, whether a spider weaving its web with exquisite skill thinks in its little head, 'I'll lay the threads in this arrangement and connect them with cross-threads. That will keep a burst of wind from shaking it to pieces. I'll make my seat where the threads originate and form a nerve center. There I'll sense whenever something hits and be able to rush to the spot. If a fly flies in, it will get tangled in the web, and I'll quickly pounce, wrap it up, and make a meal of it.'

"Consider further whether a bee thinks in its little head, 'I'll fly away. I know where flowers grow in the fields, and I'll suck wax out of some of the blossoms there and honey out of others. I'll use the wax for building cells in a network—a design that allows my coworkers and me to come and go freely along the "streets." Later, we'll stock the cells with heaping quantities of honey—enough to keep us alive even through the coming winter.' Not to mention other remarkable activities in which they not only compete with humans for political and administrative wisdom but sometimes outshine them.[4]

---

4. Swedenborg refers here to an earlier discussion of bees at 12:7 of *True Christian Religion*.

"Consider still further whether a hornet thinks in its little head, 'I'll get together with my friends to construct a little house of thin paper and make the inner walls spiral around to form a labyrinth. At the center, we'll create a kind of gathering place with a path in and a path out. We'll devise it in such a way as to prevent any other living thing besides a member of our own race from finding the way to the center where we meet.'

"Again, consider whether a silkworm while still a caterpillar thinks in its little head, 'Now it's time to prepare myself for spinning silk so that, when I've finished, I can fly out. Then, in the sky, which I've never been able to reach before, I can romp around with a number of mates and acquire offspring for myself.' Likewise for the other kinds of larva when they crawl out of their cells to become nymphs, pupas, chrysalises, and finally butterflies. Does a fly ever have any idea of breeding with another fly in this place and not that?

"It's the same with the larger animals as it is with those tiny ones. Take birds and feathered creatures of every type: they mate, build nests, lay eggs, incubate them, hatch chicks, offer them food, raise them until they fly, and then drive them from the nest as if they disowned them. And they engage in countless other behaviors as well. It's the same with terrestrial animals too, and snakes and fish.

"Can any of you fail to see from what I've said that none of their habits results from any thinking process? And you can't have ideas without thought. The mistaken notion that animals have ideas arises from a single source: the conviction that they are just as capable of thought as human beings, the power of speech representing the only distinction between them and us."

The angel stopped and looked around. Because he saw that some of the people still could not make up their minds whether or not animals possess the power of thought, he continued his appeal. "The similarity between the behavior of beasts and humans, I can see, leaves you stuck in the delusion that animals engage in thought. Let me tell you, then, where their actions do come from.

"Every animal, every fowl, every fish, reptile, and insect has its own sort of love. That love exists on three levels—those of its animal nature, its senses, and its body—and dwells in the animal's head, in the brain. By way of the brain, the spiritual world enters directly into the animal's bodily senses and uses them to generate behavior. This explains why its physical senses are far keener than human ones.

"The influence from the spiritual world is what's called instinct, and it's called instinct because it comes into play without the use of thought. Animals display noninstinctive behavior, too, which they develop with practice.

"But the kind of love an animal possesses, which provides a channel for activity generated out of the spiritual world, is directed solely toward eating and reproducing. Animals have no eagerness for knowledge, intelligence, or wisdom, which are the means for the gradual development of love in human beings.

"You can see clearly that people also lack any inborn ideas when you consider that they aren't born with any kind of thought and where thought is absent so are ideas, since neither is possible without the other.

"Newborns provide the evidence for this, in that they can't do anything but nurse and breathe. Their ability to nurse is no innate skill but rises out of their continual sucking in the mother's womb. And they can breathe because they're alive, breath being a basic requirement for life.

"Even an infant's physical senses are extremely vague and emerge gradually through stimulation. An infant's movements, likewise, develop in stages with practice.

"During the time a baby is learning to babble words and to imitate their sound without at first any concept of their meaning, a glimmering of fantasy slowly dawns. As it sharpens, the dim rudiments of imagination are born and then of thought. Ideas form in the child at the same rate that these abilities develop, and ideas, as I've already said, are bound up with thought. So thought, which is nonexistent in the beginning, grows through education.

"To sum up, people do have ideas, but not ones that are inborn, just ones that have been shaped and formed, and these are the source of human speech and behavior."

. . . Afterward I gazed about and saw [Gottfried Wilhelm] Leibnitz and [Christian] Wolff nearby. They were concentrating on the line of reasoning put forward by the angel. At that point, Leibnitz drew closer and expressed his agreement; Wolff left, both denying and affirming what the angel had said, because his powers of judgment did not run as deep as Leibnitz's.

True Christian Religion 335

One spirit was bound for heaven, the other for hell. Swedenborg was careful to notice the differences between them.

I had the use of my inner spiritual sight—the level of vision that angels of the second-highest heaven enjoy, although at the time I was in the world of spirits—and I saw two spirits not far from me but distant from each other. One of them, I perceived, loved goodness and truth, which united him with heaven, while the other loved evil and falsity, which united him with hell.

I came forward and called them together. From the sound of their voices and from their responses, I gathered that both equally could see truth and acknowledge it once seen—in other words, could think intelligently. They were also able to settle matters of the mind to their liking and matters of the will to their pleasure. Consequently, each had a similar level of free will in the use of reason.

I observed further that this freedom of mind gave rise to an apparent clarity of vision from first (in the perceptive faculties) to last (in the eye).

But when the one who loved evil and falsity was left to think on his own, I noticed that a kind of smoke wafted up from hell and destroyed the clarity he had in his higher capacities, above the level of memory. As a result, he suffered intense darkness there, like that at midnight. Furthermore, the smoke kindled and burned as if it were on fire, and this illuminated the area of his mind below the level of memory. Accordingly, his thoughts were grotesque falsities created by the evils he loved.

On the other, in contrast—the one who loved goodness and truth—I seemed to see a gentle flame gliding down from heaven when he was left to himself. This flame illumined the area of his mind above the level of memory and that below as well, down as far as the eye. The glow from that light shone stronger and stronger as his love for goodness led him to see and think of truth.

These sights made it evident to me that every person, evil or good, has free will on the spiritual plane. They also showed me that hell sometimes blots out free will in those who are evil, while heaven intensifies and galvanizes it in the good.

Afterward, I spoke with each, starting with the one who loved evil and falsity. Following some conversation regarding his current lot, I mentioned free will, and up he blazed. "It is so insane to believe that people have free will in spiritual matters!" he cried. "What individual can acquire faith or do good on his or her own?

"Doesn't the modern clergy teach that, according to the Word, we can't obtain anything unless it's given to us from heaven? And Christ our Lord told his disciples, 'Without me, you can do nothing.'

"To these arguments I will add the fact that none of us can move a foot or hand to do anything good or move our tongue to speak any living truth. On this account, the church in the wisdom of its wisest has come to the conclusion that we can't will, understand, or think anything spiritual, or even open ourselves to the possibility of doing so, any more than a statue, a stump, or a stone could.

"The church has decided, therefore, that God, the only being with absolutely free and unlimited power, imparts faith at his pleasure. Without any effort or ability on our part, by the workings of the Holy Spirit, faith accomplishes all things, which the uneducated then attribute to the efforts of mortal beings."

Next, I talked to the other man, the one who loved goodness and truth, and following some conversation regarding his current lot, I mentioned free will. "It is so insane to deny free will in spiritual matters!" he claimed. "What individual lacks the ability to will or do good, to think or speak truth on his or her own, under inspiration from the Word and so from the Lord, who is the Word?

"After all he said, 'Produce good fruit,' and 'Believe in the light,' and also, 'Love each other' and 'Love God,' plus 'Those who hear and do my commands are the ones who love me, and I will love them.' Not to mention a thousand other verses like them throughout the Word. What would be the purpose of the Word if we could will and think and therefore do and say nothing that's commanded in it?

"If human beings lacked the power to do these things, what would there be to organized religion? It would only be a shipwreck lying at the bottom of the ocean, the captain standing at the tip of its mast shouting, 'There's nothing I can do!' while watching the other sailors put to sea in lifeboats, sails spread.

"Wasn't Adam given the freedom to eat from the tree of the

knowledge of good and evil as well as the tree of life? And since, in his freedom, he did eat from the first, the snake—hell, really—injected a cloud of smoke into his mind. As a result, he found himself thrown out of paradise and cursed. In spite of all, he still wasn't stripped of free will; it says that a cherub[5] stood guard over the path to the tree of life, because otherwise he could still have exerted the desire to eat from it."

At the end of this speech, the other, the one who loved evil and falsity, said, "The things I've been listening to have slipped my mind; what sticks with me is the case that I made. But doesn't everyone know that God alone is alive and so is the only active force? That people in themselves are dead and so are merely passive? How can such a being—essentially dead and merely passive—adopt any living or active quality?"

"The human being is an organ for receiving life," was my answer, "and God alone is Life. God pours his life into the organ and all its individual parts. In the same way, the sun pours its warmth into a tree and its individual parts.

"God grants us the gift of feeling his life in ourselves as our own. He wants us to have this sensation so that we can choose, as if on our own, to live in accordance with the laws of order, which are counted by the number of commandments in the Word. He wants us to be able to prepare ourselves to welcome his love. He does constantly balance the scales on his finger to maintain

---

5. Not a chubby baby angel, but a formidable creature of the kind described in chapter 1 of Ezekiel.

control, but he never violates free will by forcing us.

"A tree can't absorb any nutrient that the sun's warmth offers through its roots unless its individual fibers thaw and warm. Neither can the nutrients flow up from the roots unless the individual fibers radiate the warmth they've received and transfer it to the veins carrying the nutrients. People go through a similar process in receiving their vital heat from God.

"Unlike the tree, they feel that heat as their own, although it's not theirs. But to the extent that they see it as their own and not God's, while they do receive the light of life, they do not receive the warmth of love from God but the heat of love from hell. This heat is blunt. It clogs up the purer, more refined branchings of the organism, just as impurities in the blood clog up the capillaries. In this way, people turn themselves from spiritual beings into merely natural ones.

"The source of free human will lies in the sensation of life as our own and in the fact that God leaves us to feel this sensation so that a bond can form between us. This would never happen unless the bond were reciprocal, and it becomes reciprocal when we exercise our freedom under the full impression that we're acting on our own.

"If God didn't leave us this sensation, we wouldn't be human. We also wouldn't have eternal life. The reciprocal bond, you see, results from God's activity in making us human instead of bestial and also from his gift to us of life after death to eternity.

"Free will in spiritual matters is what brings this about."

After listening, the evil spirit moved off to a distance. When he did, I saw on a certain tree a flying serpent called a prester[6] offering someone a piece of the tree's fruit. In my spirit, I approached the location and saw in place of the serpent a monstrosity of a person. The face was so thoroughly covered by beard that only the nose showed. Instead of the tree, there was a burning firebrand and beside it stood the man whose mind had succumbed earlier to the cloud of smoke, the one who later had rejected free will in spiritual matters.

Suddenly, a similar cloud of smoke spread from the firebrand to envelop both. As it hid them from my view, I left. The other man, though—the one who loved goodness and truth and asserted that people do have free will in spiritual matters—accompanied me home.

True Christian Religion 504

6. A Greek word meaning a burning whirlwind.

II

The First Encounter

Swedenborg Meets a Devil

The previous episodes show Swedenborg confidently moving from experience to experience in another world. Collected documents enable us to trace early experiences that precede his published works. We find that he saw a being sitting on a block of ice. And that, as far as we can discern, was his first actual sight of a devil. Let us look back at the record.

Prior to the time of his open conversations with angels and spirits, Swedenborg seems to have had concepts typical of the people of his time. We can see this from a collection of notes he wrote down upon awakening from dreams during the night; this diary lasted over a period of months. The notations were discovered long after Swedenborg's death and are now published under the title *The Journal of Dreams*.

In one entry in this dream diary, number 137, Swedenborg mentions a dream that he could only partly remember in which "the Evil One carried me into various deep places and bound me." In another dream, recorded in entry 159, in a moment of zeal and dedication, Swedenborg felt anger "against Satan" and wanted to overcome him "with the weapons of faith." At one of his lowest ebbs, he wrote the following, recorded entry 167: "In the morning I fell into terrible thoughts . . . that the Evil One had taken possession of me." He experienced "damnable thoughts"; but, at last, he had an inner vision of Jesus Christ, in which "I could know that the devil was gone."

It is evident that Swedenborg was like the rest of us in his inward struggles, uplifted sometimes and oppressed at other times, and he spoke as others of his time would speak of angels and the devil. Let us be clear about the distinction between being troubled by a demonic presence and having an actual, conscious encounter. Like the rest of the human race, Swedenborg went through dark and testing times, which might be ascribed to the presence of hellish influence. Quite different from this kind of depression and anxiety is the experience of having a spirit say something to you in specific reply to something you are thinking within yourself. It is one thing to hear a voice, and quite something else to realize that the voice comes from someone who knows what you are thinking

The "block of ice" encounter took place on September 21, 1744. We will quote directly what he wrote at that time, but first let us notice the way it is recorded in retrospect years later. In the *Spiritual Diary* (not published) an entry dated September 1749 reads: "Before my internal sight was opened so that I could speak with spirits, I supposed that no angel or spirit could ever understand and perceive my thoughts . . . (But) it happened once, at that time, that a spirit knew what I was thinking of, as appeared by his speaking with me in a few words." Again, in one of the published theological volumes, he alludes to the incident. It occurs in *Arcana Coelestia* 5855: "Before the way was opened to me to speak with spirits, I was of the opinion that no spirit nor angel could ever know or perceive my thoughts, because they were within me, and known to God alone. And then it once happened that I observed that a certain spirit knew what I was thinking, for he spoke with me about what I was thinking of, in a few words, and gave an indication of his presence by a certain sign. At this I was astounded, chiefly because he knew my thoughts." This significant incident is referred to yet again in section 6214 of the same work, but what did the spirit say? And can we imagine what Swedenborg had been thinking?

We go back to the year 1744. At that time, Swedenborg was concentrating on the study of the human body, and his thoughts affirmed God as the Creator of the wondrous human organism that he would call "the soul's kingdom."

At that time, he ambitiously imagined that, as a scientific writer, he could open people's minds to a spiritual view of created things. His goal, as one biographer put it, was "to disperse the clouds which darken the sacred temple of the mind and open a path to faith."[1]

Swedenborg testifies that he sometimes felt an oppressive presence when he wrote things "to which evil spirits were averse" (*Spiritual Diary* 2951).

So, on September 21, 1744, Swedenborg was deep in thought when a sinister voice snarled, "Hold your tongue, or I will beat you." He wrote, "I then saw someone sitting on a block of ice, and I was frightened." His fright, as we can tell from those later references to this incident, stemmed from the fact that the voice was responding to his own thoughts.

Swedenborg did not guess back in those early days that, in his work, he was beginning a dialogue with devils. He did not anticipate the debate (which appears in *True Christian Religion*, quoted later) in which evil spirits pour forth arguments and try to convince the very angels of heaven that there is no God.

When he saw a spirit on a block of ice, Swedenborg did not anticipate that he would be permitted later—without fear—to see into hell and to talk to its denizens. He did later notice coldness in the presence of infernal beings. Some chilled him to the marrow with their frigid presence, while they themselves were not conscious of cold, as he records in *True Christian Religion* 385:

---

1. Cyriel Sigstedt, *The Swedenborg Epic* (London: The Swedenborg Society, 1981), 167.

To me it seemed remarkable that those spirits themselves did not sense any coldness inside them, as they admitted. So I compared them to fish under the ice, which likewise feel no chill because their life and consequently their nature is inherently cold. . . . "They can be compared to mountains of pure ice torn from their places in the lands of the north wind, which float hither and thither in the ocean. Of these I have heard it said that their approach makes all the people on nearby ships shiver with cold. As a result, we can say that groups of people who commit themselves to faith without charity are like those bergs; with a little leeway, we can even call them such."

Swedenborg Learns Not to be Afraid

Although Swedenborg was surprised in his first encounters with opposition from spirits, we find that, in subsequent conversations, he learns not to be astonished or afraid. In fact, his encounters seem to be lessons to assure us of the power of divine protection. Early in his first published volume after his illumination, we read:

If the Lord stopped protecting a person at any moment, for even the smallest fraction of time, the person would instantly be destroyed; the reason is that the world of spirits is dominated by such a deadly hatred against anything having to do with love of the Lord or faith in him that words could never describe it.

The truth of this I can state with certainty because, for several years now, while still living in my body, I have mixed with spirits in the next life. Evil spirits—the worst possible, in fact—have crowded around me, sometimes numbering in the thousands, and they have been allowed to pour out their venom and harass me every way they could. Despite their efforts, they have been unable to harm the least hair on my head, so closely has the Lord guarded me.

All these years of experience have taught me well about the nature of the world of spirits. They have also taught me about the conflict that those who are undergoing spiritual rebirth have to endure in order to achieve the happiness of eternal life.

But a general description fails to provide enough information to lead anyone to full conviction, and that is why, by the Lord's divine mercy, details will be presented in the pages to come.

Arcana Coelestia 59

Protected we may be, but that does not deter evil spirits from attempting assaults from all sides. Inciting violence, especially toward the innocent, is one way that evil spirits threaten the peace and welfare of humanity. They endeavor "to break up and destroy marriages" (*Heaven and Hell* 384). Indeed, they provoke division in human relationships in their efforts to gain power.

We see in the following passage from Arcana Coelestia *an encounter with some malicious spirits and Swedenborg's argument with them about their delusions.*

Spirits of a certain type want to control everyone else and be their sole rulers. To that end, they stir up hostility, hatred, and fighting among others. With amazement I have seen the fighting they instigate. I asked who exactly they were and received the answer that they were sprits who create such commotions because they are intent on wielding supreme and solitary power. They follow the principle *divide and conquer*.

I had an opportunity to talk to them, and the first thing out of their mouths was that they ruled everyone. I was given to reply that they were out of their minds if they looked to such activities to provide them with power. . . .

I noticed that they had no conscience whatever, and that to them prudence and wisdom consisted in arousing hostility, hatred, and infighting in order to monopolize power.

"Do you know," I was allowed to ask them, "that you're now in the next life, where you'll live forever? Do you know that there are spiritual laws here which completely forbid such a course of action? As long as you lived in the world you were capable of being considered and accepted as the wise among fools, but here you're lunatics among the wise." This displeased them.

"You should realize," I went on, "that heaven consists in mutual love, love between one person and the next. This love creates order in heaven and makes it possible for so many thousands of people to be ruled as one. It's quite the opposite with you, because you pour such venom into the people around you that they breathe nothing but hatred, vengeance, and cruelty against their comrades."

"We can't be any other way than we are," they answered.

"Then you can see that everyone's life awaits him or her," I was given to reply.

Arcana Coelestia 5718

In the following account, people who had led outwardly moral lives learn that it is one's inner character that counts.

What devout person with wisdom does not want to know what will happen to him or her in the life after death? I will draw the general outlines so that such a person may know.

After death, people arrive at the realization that they are still alive and inhabiting a new world, and they hear that above that realm is heaven with its eternal joy and below is hell with its eternal suffering. All of them, when they have reached this stage, first resume the external personality that had been theirs in the previous world.

At this point, they firmly believe that they will be going to heaven, and they speak intelligently and act prudently. "We've lived morally," say some. "We've aimed for integrity. We haven't deliberately done anything wrong." Others say, "We've gone to church, attended Mass, kissed the holy icons, poured out prayers on bended knee." Still others say, "We've given to the poor, brought help to the needy, read devotional books; the Word, too." And so on.

After they've said these things, angels make their appearance. "All the things you've mentioned," they say, "are things you've done on a surface level. You don't yet know what you're like on the inside.

"You're now spirits in a body made of real substance. The spirit is your inner self. It's the part of you that thinks about the things you wish for and wishes for the things you love; and what you love is the joy of your life.

"All people as small children begin their lives focusing on external concerns. They learn to act morally and speak intelligently. When an idea of heaven and its blessings begins to dawn, they start to pray, attend church, and practice their religious traditions. Yet when evil wells up from its inborn spring, they learn to hide it in the secret folds of their minds and cunningly cover it up with false justifications, to the point where they themselves fail to recognize it as evil. And then since they've covered it up and put a layer of what you might call dust on the top, they don't bother to think about it any more except to make sure it never shows.

"The result is that people focus all their attention on leading an outwardly moral life, and, in this way, they become two-faced. They turn into sheep on the outside and wolves on the inside; they resemble a golden casket concealing poison within; they take after a person with bad breath sucking on a mint to keep bystanders from detecting the odor; they become like a rat skin that smells of balsam.

"You've said that you lived morally and pursued a course of piety. But I ask you, did you ever examine what you were like inside? Did you ever discover an appetite for revenge, extending even to murder? for indulging your lust, even to adultery? for practicing fraud, even to theft? for engaging in deceit, even to 'false witness'?

"Four of the ten commandments say, 'These things you are not to do' and the last two say 'These things you are not to covet.' Are you convinced that your inner self matches your outer self in these matters? If you do think so, perhaps you deceive yourselves."

"What is the inner self?" their listeners have replied. "Isn't it one and the same as the outer self? We've heard from our ministers that the inner being is nothing but faith. They say that piety on the lips and in the moral life is the sign of faith because it shows that faith is at work."

"The faith that leads to salvation does exist in the inner self," the angels answered. "Charity the same. They give rise in the outer self to a Christian hold on faith and Christian morality.

"But the appetites I mentioned earlier might remain in the inner being and so in the will and the thoughts (which rise out of will). If they do, it's proof that you love them deep down, even if you don't act or speak that way on the surface. Under those circumstances, evil ranks higher than good with you, and good ranks below evil. No matter how you talk with apparent under-standing or act with apparent love, in consequence, evil lies at the core and takes such appearances as a cover. Then you're like a clever chimp that apes human gestures without the least bit of sincerity.

"You know nothing about the nature of your inner self because you haven't scrutinized yourselves or followed scrutiny with repentance. In a little while, however, you'll have visual evidence of that nature, when you've shed your outer personality and come into possession of your inner one.

"When that happens, your own companions won't recognize

you any more, and neither will you yourselves. I've seen paragons of vice then look like wild animals, eyeing their neighbor savagely, burning with deadly hatred, and blaspheming God, whom outwardly they had worshiped."

These words caused a mass exodus. "You'll see what your lot in life is soon," the angels were saying all the while. "You'll be giving up your outer veneer shortly and coming into your true inner self, which is the spirit you now are."

True Christian Religion 568

Here is an insight into typical notions about immortality.

[With respect to people who consider appearances to be reality,] they think of the life that exists in a person on earth simply as being like that present in an animal. In regard to human life after death, they imagine it as a kind of living vapor that floats up out of the corpse or the grave, then sinks back down and dies.

This mad notion gives rise to the picture of spirits and angels as puffs of air; among those obliged to believe in eternal life, it fosters a similar conception of human souls. As a result, the soul is imagined to be without sight or hearing or speech, consequently to be blind, deaf, and mute, left in its own little portion of atmosphere with no more than the power of thought.

"How can the soul be anything?" such people ask. "Haven't the physical senses died along with the body? We can't take those senses back until our souls reunite with our bodies." And since they have been able to view the state of the soul after death only in terms of the physical senses, and not spiritually, they have settled firmly on this ethereal image. Otherwise, their belief in eternal life would have dissolved.

Divine Providence 310:3

I once had a conversation with some spirits about life. We said that none of us has any life inherent in ourselves; rather life is bestowed by the Lord, even though we seem to live under our own power. At first, the talk turned to the question of what life is. We said that to understand and to will are life, and since all understanding has to do with truth and all willing with good, an understanding of truth and the will to do good is life.

But some argumentative spirits started talking. There are certain spirits, you see, who have to be described as argumentative, because they are always arguing over whether a thing is so; for the most part, they are in the dark about all truth. These spirits, as I was saying, asserted that people who have no understanding of truth and no will to do good still have life and, in fact, believe that they live more fully than others. We were given to reply, however, that the life that evil people enjoy, although it does seem like life to them, is nevertheless the kind of life that is called spiritual death. They could recognize this, we said, by considering the fact that, if understanding the truth and willing good constitutes life as the Divinity confers it, then understanding falsity and willing evil cannot be life. For evil and falsity are contrary to true life.

To convince them thoroughly, we showed them what the life they possess is like. The visible form presented was that of the glimmer from a coal fire, obscured by a smoky haze. Since this is the light they see by, they cannot help supposing that the life of their own thought and their own will is the only kind of life there is.

Their error is brought out even more clearly by the fact that the light that provides an understanding of truth—the light of genuine life—is totally invisible to them. As soon as they come into that light, their own illumination becomes shadowy. It turns so dark that they can see nothing at all; neither, consequently, can they understand anything at all.

In addition, we demonstrated what the state of their life was like under those conditions by cutting off all the pleasure they gained from false ideas. (In the next life, this is accomplished by separating them from the spirits they are then associating with.) When we had done so, their faces took on a ghastly tinge, like that of a cadaver, so that you could say they were images of death.

Arcana Coelestia 4417

*From a crowd of newcomers to the spiritual world,
twelve are interviewed about their opinions on heaven and
hell, and we learn of the level of their beliefs.*

I once walked in company with angels in the world of spirits,
which is midway between heaven and hell. It is the place all
people go right after death, where they are prepared either for
heaven, if they are good, or for hell, if they are bad.

With the angels I discussed many subjects, including this:

"At night in the world that my body inhabits we see countless
stars large and small, each of them a sun transmitting only its light
to our solar system. When I saw that stars come into view in your
world as well, I figured there were as many of them there as in the
world where I am."

"That might be true," said the angels, pleased by my words.
"Sometimes each community in heaven shines like a star to the
sight of those below heaven, and the number of such communities
is past counting. They're all organized according to the different
affections that go to make up a good love. In God, those affections
are infinite, so the ones we receive from him are innumerable.

"Since he foresaw them before creation, my guess would be that
he used their number to determine the number of stars he would
provide—create—in the world of humans with physical bodies."

While we were going on in this fashion, I saw to the north a wide lane so jammed up with spirits that no two were more than a footstep apart. "Here's a path I've seen before," I told the angels, "with spirits like the troops of an army on it. I've heard that everyone departing from the natural world passes this way. The reason such a large number of spirits blankets it is that tens of thousands of people die every week, all of them crossing over into this world after death."

"That path ends in the middle of this world," added the angels, "at the spot where we now are. The terminus is in the middle because off to the east are communities of people who love God and their fellow human beings; on our left, to the west, are communities of people who oppose those loves; and straight in front [of the newcomers], to the south, are communities of people who are more intelligent than the rest. That's why recent arrivals from the natural world first land here.

"While they're here, the external personality they possessed lately in the previous world remains at the fore. After a time, they're gradually exposed to the deeper facets of their character, examined as to their true nature, and then brought to their rightful places, the good in heaven and the bad in hell."

We stood in the middle, where the path carrying the influx of spirits came to a stop. "Let's stay here awhile and talk to some of the newcomers," we said.

From those arriving, we chose twelve. Since they all had come only recently from the natural world, they had no idea they weren't still there. "What are your opinions about heaven and hell and the life after death?" we asked them.

"Our religious order stamped on me a belief that we'd live on after death," answered the first, "and that heaven and hell do exist. So I've believed that everyone who lives morally goes to heaven; and since everyone lives morally, no one goes to hell. Obviously, hell is a story made up by the clergy to keep us from leading bad lives.

"What difference does it make whether I think one way or the other about God? Thought is nothing more than a bit of foam or a bubble on the water that floats away and is gone."

"My beliefs," said the second, next to him, "are these: heaven and hell do exist, and God rules heaven, while the devil rules hell. Since they are enemies and so are opposed to each other, what one calls good the other calls evil. Anyone who pretends to be moral, who can make evil look good and good evil, is standing with one foot in each camp.

"What does it matter, then, whether I side with one master or the other, as long as that one smiles on me? People can enjoy evil just as much as virtue."

"What difference does it make to me," said the third, standing at the side of the second, "if I believe in heaven and hell? After all, who's come from there to tell us about it? If everyone lives on after death, why hasn't a single person out of that immense number returned to give us the news?"

From beside him, the fourth answered, "I'll tell you why no one has returned to give us the news. It's because when people breathe their last and die, either they turn into ghosts and disintegrate or they're like a single respiration, which is only a puff of air.

How can something like that return to talk to anyone?"

"Friends," continued the fifth, "just wait for the day of judgment. Then everyone will return to their bodies, and you'll see and talk to them, and they'll each tell the next what their fate was."

The sixth, standing just opposite, laughed. "How can the spirit—a breath of air—go back to a body that has been eaten up by worms? To its bones, baked by the sun and crumbling into dust?" he said. "How can the mummified body of an Egyptian, after being [ground up and] mixed by a druggist into an extract or emulsion, a potion or pill, return and tell anyone anything?

"If you have faith, go ahead and wait for that final day, but you'll wait through time and eternity in vain."

"If I believed in heaven and hell and consequently in life after death," the seventh said in turn, "I'd believe equally in a future life for birds and beasts. Aren't some of them just as moral and rational as human beings? But we're told that animals do *not* live on; neither, therefore, do people, I maintain. The logic is good, the second follows from the first. What is a human being but an animal?"

The eighth, standing behind the seventh, came forward. "Believe in heaven if you want to but I don't believe in hell." he said. "God is omnipotent, isn't he, and capable of saving everyone?"

The ninth shook this one's hand. "God is not only omnipotent but also full of grace," he said. "He can't send anyone to eternal hellfire. And if anyone *is* in hell, he can't do otherwise than rescue and lift that person up."

The tenth darted out of line to stand in the middle. "I don't believe in hell either," he said. "Didn't God send his Son to remove the sins of the whole world by atonement? How can the devil overcome that? And seeing that he can't, what then is hell?"

The eleventh, a priest, flared up when he heard this. "Don't you know that the ones who find salvation are those who have acquired a faith with the merit of Christ inscribed on it?" he said. "Don't you know that the ones who acquire such a faith are those whom God has chosen? Clearly the elect are designated at the Almighty's will, by his judgment as to just who is worthy. How can anyone argue with that?"

The twelfth, a political figure, remained silent. But, asked to put the crowning touch on these answers, he said, "I'm not about to express any personal conviction on heaven, hell, or the life after death, because no one knows anything about it. Even so, let's allow the priests to preach about such subjects without criticizing them, because that's the way to lay an invisible chain on the minds of the rabble, keeping them under restraint to the law and their leaders. The public welfare depends on it, doesn't it?"

All we had just heard completely stupefied us. "Even though these people are called Christians," we said among ourselves, "they aren't human or animal, but human animals."

To roust them out of their sleep, we said, "Heaven and hell do exist, and so does life after death. You'll become convinced when we fill you in on your current life condition. People have no idea in the first few days after they die that they aren't still living in the same world as before. The time in between is like sleep; and when people wake up from it, they don't feel as if they're anywhere new. The same thing is true of you today, so you've spoken the same thoughts you had in the previous world."

The angels revealed to the twelve their true situation, and they then saw that they were in another world among people they did not know. "Oh, where are we?" they cried.

"You're not in the natural world any longer but in the spiritual world," we said, "and we are angels."

"If you're angels," they said, now that they had come to, "show us heaven."

"Wait here a little while for our return," we answered; and in half an hour, we came back and found them waiting. "Follow us to heaven," we said.

They followed, and we ascended with them. Since we were accompanying them, the guards opened the gate and let them in. To those who were welcoming newcomers at the threshold we said, "Examine them."

They turned the newcomers around and saw that the backs of their heads were all hollowed out. "Get away from here," they said. "You love evildoing and take pleasure in it, so you have no connection with heaven, and this is because at heart you have denied God and spurned religion."

"Don't delay, or you'll be thrown out," we informed them. They rushed back down and took off.

On the way home, we discussed the reason that people who take delight in doing evil are hollow at the back of their heads in this world. The reason I gave was this: the human brain is divided into two major parts, one in back called the cerebellum and one in front called the cerebrum. The love present in the will occupies the cerebellum, while the thought present in the intellect occupies the cerebrum. When thought (the intellect) fails to guide love (the will) in a person, the deepest regions of the cerebellum—which in themselves belong to heaven—cave in, leaving a hollow.

True Christian Religion 160

III

The Nature of Devils and of Hell

Although Swedenborg usually speaks of those in hell as "evil spirits," he reports, as we have already seen, that they were previously people living in the natural world. How, then, did these people end up in hell? Unlike other theologies, which envision a wrathful God who punishes the wicked, Swedenborg states quite plainly that "the Lord casts no one into hell: spirits cast themselves down." If "hell" is a place of suffering we naturally want to avoid, it seems strange that anyone would choose hell. But to Swedenborg, hell essentially is a state of mind and spirit—a reflection of one's own heart or inner spirit. If one chooses to be in a malicious, vengeful state of mind, one chooses to be "in hell." To quote Swedenborg, in *Heaven and Hell* 545:

60

Some people are persuaded that the Lord turns his face away from us, casts us away from himself and into hell, and is angry with us because of our evil. Some people are even persuaded that God punishes and does evil to us. . . .

Anyone whose mind is enlightened perceives . . . the fact that God is Good itself, Love itself, and Mercy itself, the Good being incapable of doing evil to anyone, Love and Mercy being incapable of casting a person away from themselves because this goes against the essential nature of mercy and love and therefore against the Divine itself.

How, then, does someone end up in hell? Swedenborg explains in *Heaven and Hell* 548. Since, in a sense, a person who loves evil is already in hell while he is living in the natural world, it is natural that he should seek his true home after death, a place where he can be with other spirits of the same ilk. After death, when the evil spirit enters the other life,

he is at first welcomed by angels who do everything for him—talk with him about the Lord, heaven, and angelic life, and give him instruction in matters of truth and goodness. But if this person, now a spirit, is the kind who had in fact known these things in the world, but had denied them at heart or sneered at them, then after some conversation he craves and tries to get away. When the angels detect this they leave him.

After he has been with other people for a while, he eventually joins in with people who are involved in the same kind of evil as he. . . . When this takes place, the person turns away from the Lord, and turns his face toward the hell he had been bonded to in the world, where there are people involved in his own kind of love of what is evil.

Doesn't a "judgment" occur, and is there not a "book of life" out of which people are judged? The "book of life," says Swedenborg, is not written on paper; it is written upon our hearts and spirits. Everything one has thought and done can be reproduced from the memory, as if it were read in a book. The reason the memory or book of life needs to be "opened" in certain cases is that there are people who are habitual deniers, skilled in covering up what they are really like. Swedenborg recounts what he witnessed, in *Heaven and Hell* 462a:

> There were some people who denied crimes and disgraceful things they had committed in the world. So lest people believe them innocent, all things were uncovered and reviewed out of their memory, in sequence, from their earliest age to the end. . . .
>
> There were some people who had taken others in by evil devices and who had stolen. Their wiles and thefts were recounted one after another—many of them things hardly anyone in the world had known other than the thieves themselves. . . .
>
> There were people who took bribes and made a profit out of judicial decisions. These people were examined from their memory in similar fashion, and from this source everything they had done from the beginning to the end of their tenure of office was reviewed. There were details about how much and what kind, about the time, about the state of their mind and intent, all cast together

in their remembrance, now brought out into sight. . . .

There were people who had lured virgins into dishonor and had violated chastity, who were called to a similar judgment. . . . The actual faces of the virgins and other women were produced just as thought they were there, with the locales, the voices, the moods. This was just as immediate as when something is presented to the sight. Sometimes these demonstrations lasted for some hours.

There was one person who thought nothing of disparaging others. I heard his disparaging remarks repeated in their sequence, his defamations as well, in the actual words—whom they were about, whom they were addressed to. . . .

There was a particular person who had robbed a relative of his inheritance by some crafty device. . . . This same person, shortly before his death, had secretly killed a neighbor by poison. . . . Then everything was unveiled—how the poisoner had talked with him as a friend and had offered him a drink, then what he had planned beforehand and what happened afterwards. . . .

In short, evil spirits are shown clearly all their evil deeds, crimes, thefts, deceits, and devices. These are brought out of their own memories and proven; there is no room left for denial, since all the attendant circumstances are visible at once.

Even still, a spirit is not sentenced to hell as a result of evil deeds done in the world, for he or she may repent of evil and choose good. Those who are in hell have turned away from the choice of good.

The "devils" in hell seem to themselves to be just as they were while living on earth, even to the point of keeping their earthly appearance. Or so it seems to them, since God, in his mercy, does not want them to suffer more than their evil state necessitates. Yet, to an angel—and certainly to Swedenborg—they appear to be hideous. As Swedenborg puts it, they look one way "in their own light"—in the delusion-producing atmosphere of hell—and another way in true light. While living on earth, people may appear outwardly beautiful, even though their spirit is not beautiful at all. "I have been shown this occasionally," he writes in *Heaven and Hell* 131. He saw people who had been charming in appearance but who became, after death, quite repulsive to behold, "while in others not beautiful there was a spirit beautifully formed, pure, and angelic." He goes on to say, "And, wonderful to tell, while those in hell appear to one another as people, *in the light of heaven*, they appear with a horrid face," even as monsters.

The change in outward appearance is gradual. People after death are in what Swedenborg calls a state of exteriors. In this state, which he reports is called the "world of spirits," the newly dead can be recognized by other spirits who knew them when they were alive. But this state is temporary. Swedenborg saw people in this state whom he had known, and he recognized them; but when he saw the same people with their true nature revealed, it was a different story. In *Heaven and Hell* 457, he explains how this happens:

> I have seen some people just arrived from the world, and
> recognized them by face and voice; but when I saw them later, I did

not recognize them. The ones who were involved in good affections had beautiful faces, while the ones who were involved in evil affections had misshapen faces. Seen in its own right, a person's spirit is nothing but his affection: its outer form is his face.

Another reason faces change is that people in the other life are not allowed to feign affections which do not really belong to them. That is, they are not allowed to put on a face contrary to the love they are engaged in. Absolutely everyone there is resolved into a state in which he speaks the way he thinks, and displays in his expression and gestures what his intentions are.

We might also add here that the dress of evil spirits matches their ugly exterior. In *Heaven and Hell* 182, Swedenborg records that "people in hell, lacking truths, are . . . clothed . . . in torn, dirty, offensive clothes, each in accord with his folly. They can wear nothing else."

The Gnashing of Teeth

What about the speech of evil spirits? The book *Heaven and Hell* has dozens of chapters about heaven and its wonders, and sometimes the final few lines of a chapter will say something about the same thing as it applies to those in hell. The chapter dealing with the way angels speak talks about the charming nature of their verbal expression. Speech reflects one's inward loves; since the angels have such good affections, "we can see how choice and pleasant their conversation is. It actually touches not just the ears, but the more inward reaches of the minds of those who hear it," we learn in *Heaven and Hell* 238. As one might expect, the chapter concludes by saying that the speech of the evil "comes from dirty concepts, which angels wholly spurn. . . . To angels, hellish speech is like a foul smell. . . . The speech itself [of evil spirits] sounds like a grinding of teeth, and strikes horror."

The "gnashing of teeth" is a phrase familiar to readers of the Bible, who rightly associate it with the plight of the evil and with hell fire (for example, in Matthew 8 and 13, and Luke 13:28). One of the few chapters of *Heaven and Hell* that deal directly with the nature of hell is entitled "What Hell-Fire and Gnashing of Teeth Are," chapter 59. Here Swedenborg testifies that, rather than referring to an actual fire, hell fire means

> a craving to do evil things that come from self-love and love of the world, and since all the people in the hells have this kind of craving, when the hells are opened one can see something fiery, with smoke, the sort of thing one sees in great conflagrations. There is something fiery from the hells where self-love rules, and something flame-like from the hells where love of the world rules. . . .
>
> It should however be noted that the people who are in the hells are not "in fire"—the fire is an appearance. They are not in fact conscious of any burning there, only of the same kind of warmth they felt before, in the world.

As for the "gnashing of teeth," we find that is the continual contention and combat of false notions. Since everyone in hell struggles on behalf of his or her own particular variety of falsehood and calls it truth, there is constant enmity between the inhabitants of hell. Outside of hell, this warfare sounds like the gnashing of teeth.

There are, nonetheless, torments in hell, although Swedenborg declares that God does not torment or inflict pain. Selfish people are inclined to torment each other, and they love to administer punishment. Since hell is the abode of those who particularly love to dominate others, you can imagine that one of the chief delights of evil spirits is tormenting other spirits. However, God ensures that punishments will only happen when they are productive of some good or when they return someone from a state of disorder to a state of order.

The fear of punishment is necessary in the communities of hell. The Lord is said to send angels to hell to restrain from any excessive punishment, and those angels by their very presence moderate the disturbances and insanities of hell, as he relates in *Heaven and Hell* 543.

There are two aspects of heaven—love and wisdom—and there are two aspects of hell—evil and falsity. A general dichotomy Swedenborg observes is that those who delight in evil may be called "devils." Just take the "d" off, and the word becomes "evil." Those whose emphasis is on what is false may be called "satans" (*Apocalypse Explained* 535). Another generalization of terms is that those who are obsessed with the world and its pleasures may be called "satans," while those in the conceit of self-love and in the lust of dominating are called "devils" (*Apocalypse Explained* 1142).

Swedenborg does not enumerate different "species" of devils. The variety among evil spirits might be compared with the variety among criminals. Some are thieves, and some are into brutality, and so forth. Regardless of terms Swedenborg may use, the reference is not to some mythological, fallen, winged creature but to a human being who has chosen hell. Sometimes manipulative female spirits are referred to as "sirens," as conniving male spirits may be referred to as "magicians." What about things like "satyrs"? Swedenborg says that, in the spiritual world, someone seen at a distance can take on a symbolic appearance that indicates that individual's nature. A common example is that the angels of the highest heaven are typically seen at a distance as if they were little children. When they come nearer, they are seen to be adults. Similarly, evil spirits may appear at a distance in different forms. Swedenborg saw at a distance "satyrs," beings with cloven hooves who are particularly lascivious. When he spoke to them first hand, he saw that they were men.

The nature of the evil spirit who turns away from God is malicious; but, in hell, there are seeming alliances, for one spirit favors another if personal advantage can be achieved thereby. In *Heaven and Hell* 574, we learn that

> As a spirit . . . comes willing or out of his own freedom to his hell and enters it, he is received warmly at first and believes that he has arrived among friends. However, this lasts only a few hours. During this time, he is being examined to determine how clever he is and therefore how strong he is. Once this examination is finished, they begin to attack him in various ways, progressively more sharply and violently. This is achieved by leading him farther and

more deeply into hell, for the farther and deeper one goes into hell, the more vicious the spirits.

The world beyond this world has its objects and its scenery. Indeed, Swedenborg reports that not only do the homes of angels reflect the inward nature of the angels who live there but even the plants and surroundings do so. While we mention angels here, bear in mind that this would apply in its own way to devils. It is almost as if the surroundings of angels emanated from their inner nature. What is outside an angel "corresponds" to what is inside the angel. But this is subtle and not really obvious. One of Swedenborg's paragraphs on this subject concludes with the following lines. "It has been granted me to perceive that angels, when their eyes were opened by the Lord, and they saw these things from the correspondence of their uses, recognized and saw themselves therein" (*Divine Love and Wisdom* 322).

So, if one's surroundings reflect one's inner nature, one may conclude the nature of the surroundings of evil spirits. However, there is an important distinction. Just as the outward appearance of an evil spirit is different when seen in the light of heaven, so the scenes of hell are different depending on who beholds them. We may speak of hell as a kingdom of darkness, but Swedenborg says that evil spirits have their own kind of light. (He uses the Latin word *lumen* for this, rather than the usual one, *lux*.) It is a matter of mercy that evil spirits see themselves and their surroundings in their own light, for when the light of heaven shines on them, the ugliness is plain to see. Swedenborg says that he was permitted to see hell's ugly scenes in heaven's light. He spoke of barren deserts, of fearful forests, of dirty streets and pathetic dwellings in *Heaven and Hell,* chapter 61, particularly section 586. To quote:

> Some hells give the visual appearance of caverns and caves in the rocks, leading inward and then on into the depths, obliquely and vertically. Some hells give the visual appearance of the kind of lairs and dens wild beasts live in, in forests. . . .
>
> In some hells, one can see something like the rubble of homes or cities after a great fire, where hellish spirits live and hide. In milder hells one sees something like tumbledown huts, crowded together rather like a city, with sections and streets. Within the houses are hellish spirits, so there are constant brawls, hostilities, beatings, and clawings. There are robberies and hold-ups in the streets and districts.
>
> In some hells there is nothing but brothels that look disgusting and are full of all kinds of filth. . . .

Punishment in Hell

Hell is considered by some to be God's revenge or punishment. Swedenborg says that God does not seek revenge or inflict punishment. God is constantly acting in mercy towards everyone, and that includes everyone in hell. Although God permits people to choose a hellish life, he works with them "bending them towards a milder hell." Swedenborg writes in *Arcana Coelestia* 6489: "Nothing is permitted except for the end that some good may come out of it, but as people have freedom, in order that they may be reformed, they are bent from evil to good so far as they suffer themselves to be bent in freedom, and [if they cannot be led to heaven] continually from the most atrocious hell into a milder one."

God never punishes us. He makes the sun rise on the evil and on the good and sends rain on the just and the unjust. He is "kind to the unthankful and evil" (Luke 6:35).

However, evil does have its consequences, and just as a life of kindness is its own reward, a life of evil carries with it its own punishment. Swedenborg uses fire as an example. If you put your hand in it, you will feel consequences, but the fire is not to blame; and neither is God to blame. The same is true of spiritual fires, the evil passions of hate, lust, and selfishness.

The Bible does speak of the wrath of God, but Swedenborg says that love only appears wrathful to the wicked, and so it should. We tend to think from a model of reward and punishment. Suppose someone does good deeds and plays by the rules or professes certain beliefs for a number of years. Is everlasting bliss a kind of payment or reward for that? On the other hand, if one acts or believes wrongly, will there be a repayment of everlasting torment?

While a concept of reward can motivate us towards what is right, eventually we find that the "reward" is in the doing of good. According to Psalm 19, we have precepts from God and "in keeping them there is great reward." "Great reward" is a phrase used in an intriguing passage in Luke. Here we are told to do good "hoping for nothing in return," and then comes the saying "and your reward shall be great" (Luke 6:35). Doing good without hope of reward carries within it great reward. Swedenborg says that the feeling one gets in doing good with no thought of reward is "so great" that it may be called heaven itself, and devils just cannot comprehend it (*Arcana Coelestia* 6391). We see the converse in hypocrites. Jesus said not to be like them: "I say to you, they have their reward" (Matt. 6:2). Their reward is to be a hypocrite. A message of devils to Swedenborg was in effect, "We are what we are." And they were seen to be fools.

Foolish Delusions

C. S. Lewis prefaced his book *The Screwtape Letters* with two short quotations. He cited Thomas Moore's observation that "the devil cannot endure to be mocked," and he quoted the following saying of Martin Luther: "The best way to drive out the devil, if he will not yield to texts of Scripture, is to jeer and flout him, for he cannot bear scorn."

The derision of fools is one of the themes of the Bible. The shortest of Jesus' parables is: "Can the blind lead the blind? Will they not both fall into the ditch?" (Luke 6). Jesus derided the Pharisees as "blind leaders of the blind" who end up in the ditch (Matt. 15:14). "Blind guides," chided Jesus, "who strain out a gnat and swallow a camel!" (Matt. 23:24). Comical imagery of tumbling into a ditch or swallowing a camel is a portrayal of an utter fool. One of the purposes of Scripture is to take the vain thoughts of man and reduce them to their absurdity. The calculating man schemes inwardly to build greater barns and amass wealth. "But God said to him, 'You fool! This night your soul will be required of you; then whose will those things be which you have provided?'" (Luke 12:20).

"To do evil is like sport to a fool," says the book of Proverbs, which time and again and from all sorts of angles portrays to us the ways of a fool. The numerous references to fools and foolishness in Proverbs sometimes seems like merely common-sense advice. To act imprudently will not serve you well. It is counterproductive to be foolish. But the term *fool* in Scripture is used in sinister ways. The way of evil is the way of foolishness. The contention of a wise man with a foolish man (as in Proverbs 29:9) is very much a part of the subject of debates with devils.

The denial of God is characteristic of the denizens of hell. One of the messages from hell for the human heart is that God does not exist. Both Psalms 14 and 53 open by declaring what the fool says in his heart, which is that, "There is no God." And along with the negation of God, there is the characteristic of self-aggrandizement, of boastfulness.

It is interesting to see that one of the words translated "fool" in the Old Testament is actually a word which means one who boasts. Whereas the King James will say, "I said unto the fools, Deal not foolishly," revised versions render it, "I say to the boastful, do not boast" (Psalm 75:4). Foolishness and boastfulness are typical characteristics of the evil spirits which Swedenborg encountered. We find in Swedenborg stories of people proud of their erudition. Seemingly brilliant, they turn out to be nothing but fools inwardly.

Another Hebrew word that is rendered "fool" is a word that means "self confident." (Examples of this word include Psalms

49:10, 92:6, 94:8). Swedenborg from personal experience testifies that those who have trust or confidence in themselves alone are seen in the other life to "speak idiotically, for they are in stupidity" (*Arcana Coelestia* 4532). Says Swedenborg, "It has been granted me to speak with many of the learned after their departure from the world. . . . Those who in heart had denied the Divine had become so stupid as to have little comprehension even of civic truth, still less of anything spiritual" (*Heaven and Hell* 354). In the same book, Swedenborg speaks of some who had enjoyed an impressive retention of facts but who were found to be utterly foolish (*Heaven and Hell* 464). While they were shown to be foolish, he observes, "yet they seemed to themselves to be wiser than others" (*Heaven and Hell* 506). A theme of Scripture is that "it is better to trust in the Lord than to put confidence in man" (Psalm 118:8).

Let us look at a sequence of adventures involving boastful devils acclaimed for their brilliance. Notice at one point that they are portrayed as if they are stamping on one spot of ground. It brought a smile to the faces of attending angels when Swedenborg commented that they had better be careful lest they dig a hole in the dirt!

"Oh how brilliant they are," cries a multitude.

I once heard some shouting, as if it bubbled up from below through water. One cry—"How just they are!"—came from the left, one from the right—"How brilliant!"—and the third—"How wise!"—from behind. It entered my mind to wonder whether there were just, brilliant, and wise people even in hell and accordingly I felt a desire to see. "You will see and hear," I heard from heaven.

I left home in the spirit and saw an opening in front of me. Approaching it, I looked down and there before my eyes was a stairway. Down I went. At the bottom I saw stretches of ground thick with scrub and a sprinkling of prickers and nettles. "Is this hell?" I asked.

"This is a lower region just above hell," they said.

I followed a course that took me to the source of each shout in order. At the site where the first cry—"How just!"— originated, I saw a group of those who in the world had been judges tainted by favoritism and bribery. At the site of second—"How brilliant!"—I saw a group of those who in the world had engaged in argument. And at the source of the third—"How wise!"—I saw a group of those who in the world had spent time constructing proofs.

But I turned back from this last set to the first, the judges tainted by favoritism and bribery and proclaimed as equitable. I saw to one side a kind of amphitheater made of brick and roofed with black tile. Someone told me that this was their courthouse. Three entrances opened into it from the north and three from the west but none from the south or east—a sign that their verdicts were based not on justice but on whim.

In the middle of the amphitheater, I saw a hearth and fire-tenders throwing on burning logs saturated with sulfur and tar. The light given off, shimmering on the plastered walls, threw up silhouettes of the birds that inhabit dusk and nightfall. But the hearthplace and the unsteady light that formed those images existed to represent the judges' decisions and the way in which they could falsely color the dispute in any controversy, laying on it whatever appearance suited their prejudice.

After half an hour, I saw the entrance of elders and young adults clad in robes and gowns who took off their hats and settled on the imposing chairs at the bench, ready to sit in judgment. Now I heard and perceived how skillfully, how cleverly they could avoid the appearance of favoritism and convert their judgments into seeming justice. They were so good at it that they themselves could not help seeing injustice as justice and vice versa. It was visible in their faces and audible in the sound of their voices that these were their convictions about the merits of the cases.

Then enlightenment from heaven came to me and showed me whether each ruling was legitimate or not. I saw how much energy the judges used to hide what was unfair and give it a mask of fairness. I saw them choose out those laws that favored them, bend the controversy in that direction, and shove all the rest off to the side through ingenious argument.

After they handed down their decisions, their opinions were relayed to their supporters, friends, and allies outside, who repaid them for their favor by walking far down the road shouting, "How just they are! How just!"

I discussed these things with some angels from heaven, telling them a part of what I had seen and heard. "Judges like these appear to others as though they were gifted with the keenest intellects," said the angels. "But the truth is that they're completely blind to justice and fairness. If you take away friendship for another, they sit in court like statues. All they can say is, 'I yield. I agree with this person or that.'

"The reason is that all their judgment is prejudgment or prejudice, and prejudice, with its favoritism, dogs their trials from beginning to end. Consequently, they see nothing but what favors their friends. Whenever a thing opposes their interests, they divert their gaze and look out the corner of their eyes at it. If they take it up again, they tangle it in arguments like a spider wrapping its prey in silk and devour it.

"The result is that if they can't follow their own prejudices as guidelines, they can't form a vision of right and wrong. They've been examined on this point and found incapable. The inhabitants of your world will be incredulous, but tell them it's a truth tested by the angels of heaven.

"As they're completely blind to justice, we in heaven don't consider them human beings but monstrous imitations. Bias forms the head of the monster, injustice the torso, and supporting arguments the hands and feet. Any question of justice is relegated to the soles of the feet where, if it fails to cater to bias, one can trip it up and trample on it.

"But you're about to see what they're like essentially; their end is at hand."

Suddenly, the earth yawned open! Bench fell on bench. The people were swallowed up, together with the whole amphitheater, and were thrown into caves and imprisoned. "Do you want to see them there?" I was asked. Amazing to see, their faces looked as if they were made of polished steel, their bodies from neck to hip as if they were pieces of sculpture draped in leopard skins, and their feet as if they were snakes. I saw their law books, formerly lying on the benches, changed into playing cards. Now instead of handing down judgments, they won the job of processing vermilion for rouge to coat the faces of prostitutes and turn them into beauties.

When these sights came to an end, I wanted to visit the two other groups—the one containing people who could only argue and the one containing those who could only demonstrate proofs. "Wait a little," I heard. "You'll get some angel companions from the community directly above them. They'll bring light from the Lord to you, and you'll see astounding things."

A little later, I heard from below ground the same voices as before—"How brilliant they are! How brilliant!"—and I looked around to see who was there. My gaze fell on some angels from the heaven directly above the people shouting, "How brilliant!"

I spoke with them about the shouting. "The great scholars

you're hearing about," they said, "are people who can do no more than argue whether an idea is true or not. Rarely do they think, 'This is so.'

"They're like gusts of wind that blow through and are gone. They're like tree bark without the living core, like almond shells without the nut, like fruit peels without the flesh. Their minds lack any depth of judgment and are connected only to the bodily senses. If the actual senses don't pass judgment on a thing, such people are unable to draw any conclusion concerning it.

"In short, their thinking rises no higher than the senses, and we call them debaters. We call them that because they never come to a decision. Instead, they take up any proposition they hear and argue about its validity, constantly disagreeing. They love nothing more than attacking the truth and tearing it to shreds by subjecting it to disputation.

"These are the ones who consider themselves scholars more brilliant than everyone else in the world."

I asked the angels to lead me to them. They took me to a cave with steps reaching down into a lower region. I descended and followed the sound of the shouting, "How brilliant!" And there were several hundred people standing in one place, stamping on the dirt! "Why are you standing there beating the ground with your feet?" I asked in amazement.

"If you keep it up, you'll dig a hole in the dirt," I added.

The angels smiled at this. "They look as though they're standing there like that because they have no thought that a given statement is true," said the angels. "They only *ask* whether it's true and wrangle over it. Since their thinking goes no further, they seem to just wear away a single clod of dirt by trampling it without moving on.

"People arriving in this world from the natural world who hear that they've entered another existence gather in clusters in many places," the angels continued. "They ask where heaven and hell are and where God is. After receiving instruction, they still start in on arguing, debating, and disputing whether there is a God.

"They do so because a lot of people in the natural world nowadays revere nature. When conversation turns to religion, these people bring the topic up for debate among themselves and with others. The debate they propose in this way almost never ends in the affirmative for a belief in God.

"As time passes, these nature-worshipers ally themselves more and more with the evil, because no one can do good out of a love of goodness unless motivated by God."

Later I was led to a gathering and, to my surprise, saw people whose faces were not ugly and whose clothes were elegant. "That's what they look like in their own light," said the angels. "But if light from heaven enters in, their faces change and their clothes too." So it happened. Now their faces looked dark, and they seemed to be wearing black sackcloth; but as soon as heaven's light receded, they appeared the same as before.

Then I talked to some of those gathered. "I heard the crowd around you shouting 'How brilliant!'" I said. "Let's converse, then, on topics of the highest scholarship."

"Say whatever you wish," they replied, "and we'll satisfy you."

"What kind of religion leads to salvation?" I asked.

"We will subdivide this inquiry into several individual questions," they said. "Until we've reached a conclusion on them, we cannot give you a response. Now, the deliberations will be:

1. Is religion anything?
2. Is there such a thing as salvation or not?
3. Is one religion more effective than another?
4. Do heaven and hell exist?
5. Is there life after death to eternity?

And many more."

I asked about the first one—whether religion is anything. They delved into it with a wealth of arguments. I requested that they turn it over to the larger group, and they complied. The unanimous answer was that the proposition required more investigation than could be completed by evening.

"Can you finish in a year?" I asked.

"Not in a hundred years," said one.

"In the meantime, you have no religion," I said. "And since salvation depends on religion, you have no conception of salvation, no belief in it, and no hope for it."

"Don't we have to demonstrate first whether there is such a thing as religion, what it is, and whether it's anything?" the same one answered. "If it is anything, it must exist even for the more sage among us. If not, it must exist for the masses alone. Everyone knows that religion is called a restraint, but the question is, on whom? If it's intended only for the masses, it's not really anything; but if it's binding on the wise as well, it is."

"If there's anything you're not, it's brilliant," I said on hearing this. "Your thinking goes no further than to ask whether a thing exists and to examine the question from both sides. How can anyone be erudite without knowing something for certain? Without making progress in it—the same way a person makes physical, step-by-step progress—until gradually arriving at wisdom? Otherwise, you don't touch on truths with even the nail of your finger but thrust them further and further out of sight.

"Arguing merely over whether a thing exists is like arguing about a hat or shoe that you never try on. What comes of it? Only a failure to see whether it does exist, whether it's any more than an idea. Only a failure to tell whether there's such a thing as salvation, life after death to eternity, one religion that stands out over another, or a heaven and hell. You can't begin to think about them as long as you're stuck beating the sand at the first step, refusing to set one foot firmly down after the other in order to get somewhere.

"Watch out, or while you're stalling this way outside the hall of judgment, your minds will calcify inside you, and you'll become pillars of salt."

With these words, I left. In their consternation, they threw stones after me; and at that point, they looked to me like carved images containing not a whit of human reason.

I asked the angels what would happen to them. "The worst ones sink far down into a wasteland where they're forced to carry heavy loads," they said. "There, because they can't produce anything rational, they babble meaningless nonsense. At a distance, they look like donkeys bearing a burden."

Next, one of the angels said, "Follow me to the place where they're shouting 'How wise!'

"You'll see some freakish beings," he added. "You'll see faces and bodies that are human and yet are not."

"Are they animals then?" I asked.

"Not animals," he answered, "but animal-humans. You see, they have no ability to tell whether the truth is true or not but still can give an appearance of truth to anything they want. With us, people like this are called proof-givers."

Seeking out the shouts, we arrived at the proper place, where we found a group of men surrounded by a crowd. Certain members of the crowd were of noble lineage; and when they heard the men delivering proofs of all they said and agreeing with them with such manifest partiality, they turned around and said, "How wise!"

"Let's not approach them," the angel said to me. "Let's call one member of the group over here."

We did as he said and took the man aside. We made various statements, and he corroborated every one of them, going so far as to give them the full appearance of truth. We asked him whether he could also prove the reverse. "Just as thoroughly as the first," he declared. And then he said openly and from the heart, "What is truth? Is there anything in the universe that's true unless a person makes it true? Say whatever you please and I'll make it true."

"Make it true that faith is the beginning and end of the church," I suggested. He did so with such great ability and skill that those scholars standing by expressed admiration and applauded. Then I entreated him to make it true that charity is the beginning and end of the church, and he did; I asked him to make it true that charity has nothing to do with the church, and he dressed up both propositions and tricked them out with fancy appearances, so that the bystanders looked at each other and said, "Isn't he wise?"

"Don't you know," I asked, "that living as we ought is charity and believing as we ought is faith? Don't those who live as they ought also believe as they ought? Undoubtedly, the conclusion is that faith is bound up with charity and charity with faith. Don't you see this is true?"

"I'll make it true and see," he answered, and that is what he did. "Now I see it," he said. But immediately he made the opposite true, and then he said, "I see that this is true too."

"Aren't they contradictory?" we said, smiling at this. "How can two contrary statements be seen as true?"

"You're wrong," he answered, annoyed. "Both are true, because nothing else is true but what a person makes true."

Standing near was a man who had been a top-level ambassador in the world. "I admit," he said, amazed at what he was hearing, "that something of the kind can be asserted in the world, but you're still out of your mind. Make it true, if you can, that light is darkness and darkness light."

"Easily," returned the other. "What are light and dark but conditions of the eye? Doesn't light turn to shadow when we come in on a bright day, or when we stare at the sun? Everyone knows that our eyes change then, seeing light as shade. And, of course, when the eye recovers, what had seemed to be shade looks in its turn like light.

"Doesn't an owl see the dark of night as the light of day and vice versa? Then again, it sees even the sun as nothing but a dim and dusky globe. If we had eyes like an owl's, which would we call light and which dark?

"What then is light but a condition of the eye? If so, isn't light darkness and darkness light? Consequently since one is true, so is the other."

As this proof confused some listeners, I said, "That proof-giver, I noticed, doesn't realize that both true light and false are possible, or that both kinds seem bright. False light is *not* actually light, though. Compared to the genuine thing, it's darkness.

"An owl uses false light because at the back of its eye lies the desire to chase and devour other birds, and false light allows its eye to see at night. Cats are exactly the same; in a cellar, their eyes look like candles. What produces the effect is false light emanating from the desire to chase and devour mice, which lurks in their eyes.

"Obviously, then, sunlight is true light and desire's light is false."

Now the ambassador asked the proof-giver to make this true: a crow is white, not black. "I'll do that easily too," he answered.

"Take a needle or razor and cut open the outer feathers and down feathers on a crow. Then remove all the feathers and look at the crow's skin. Isn't it white? What's the black on the outside but a shadow? That's nothing to judge the color of a crow by!

"If you want to know whether black is just a shadow, ask the optical experts, and they'll tell you. Or grind a black stone or a piece of black glass into a fine powder, and you'll see that the powder is white."

"Isn't a crow black to the sight?" replied the ambassador.

"Would you, a rational being, base your thoughts on appearances?" answered the proof-giver. "It's true that appearances could lead you to say a crow is black, but you can't think it!

"You can say on the basis of appearances that the sun rises and sets, to take an example. But as a human being you can't think that way, since the sun stands still and the earth moves. It's the same with a crow. Appearances are only appearances. Say what you will, a crow is white through and through. It even turns white as it ages; I've seen it happen."

At this, the bystanders turned to gaze at me. "It's true," I said, "that crow feathers from both layers are whitish, and the skin the same. That's true, though, not only with crows but with all the birds in the world! Every rational being uses apparent color to tell birds apart. If we didn't, we'd be calling every bird white, which is absurd and pointless."

The ambassador inquired whether the man could make it true that he himself was insane. "I can, but I don't want to," he said. "Who isn't insane?"

Then they asked him to say from the heart whether he was joking or whether he really believed that there is no truth but what a person makes true. "I swear I believe it," he answered.

After all this, the Man Who Could Prove Anything was sent to some angels to have them explore his character. "He doesn't possess even a grain of intellect," they said when done. "With him, everything above the rational level is shut tight. Only the parts below it are open.

"Spiritual light exists above the rational level, and natural light exists below. Natural light in humans is such that it lets them back any position they choose. If spiritual light doesn't flow down into the natural light, a person can't discern the truth of a true statement or, consequently, the falsity of a false one. The ability to see both comes as a result of the spiritual light shining from within the natural. And spiritual light comes from the God of heaven, who is the Lord.

"So the Man Who Can Prove Anything is not human or animal but an animal-human."

I asked the angels about the fate of such people. "Can they coexist with the living?" I said. "Spiritual light is the source of human life and of human intellect."

"When people of this type are by themselves," they said, "they can't think a single thought. So they can't speak a single word either. They stand like unspeaking robots or as if they were in a deep sleep. As soon as their ears catch hold of a sound, however, they wake up.

"They get that way," added the angels, "because deep down they're evil. No spiritual light can flow into them from above. The only 'spiritual' influence they receive comes by way of the world, and it gives them the ability to construct proofs."

After these words a message from the angels who had exam-

ined him came to my ears. "Draw a conclusion that covers all
you've heard," it said.

This was the conclusion I came to: the ability to prove whatever you want is not a mark of intelligence. The ability to see truth
as true and falsity as false, and to prove it, is.

Then I looked over to where the proof-givers stood surrounded by a crowd exclaiming, "How wise!" Suddenly, a murky
cloud hid them, with screech owls and bats flitting about in it.

"The owls and bats flying around in the cloud exist because
they correspond to the thoughts of those people," someone told
me; "they *are* those thoughts in visible form.

"The practice of arguing so persuasively for falsities that they
come to seem true is represented in this world in the form of night
birds, their eyes lit from within by false light, which see objects
lying in the dark as if they were in the light. The same false light,
.in a spiritual version, shines for people who argue on behalf of
falsity until it seems to be truth and afterwards believe it to be
true. Such people can all see a thing *a posteriori*; they can't see
anything *a priori*."

True Christian Religion 332–334

IV
Hell's Paradoxical Cunning

We have spoken of devils as clumsy fools, and in a moment, we will talk of their awesome cunning. It is a kind of paradox. Their bumbling stupidity may be compared with recent observations about the mentality of criminals. There have been television specials about America's dumbest criminals, and millions have been entertained by stories of bungling bank robbers and incompetent thieves.

A landmark study in the area was *The Criminal Personality*, published in 1976. The authors, Samuel Yochelson and Stanton Samnenow, observed that criminals often have especially short attention spans. They are frequently lazy mentally as well as physically. They may not easily recognize the similarity between situations and may fail to learn by experience. When they engage in some enterprise and one or two things go wrong, their errors tend to increase geometrically with results that provide law-abiding citizens with mirth as well as reassurance.

A particularly entertaining presentation of this subject has been provided by Chuck Shepherd in a little book called *America's Least Competent Criminals*.[1] Here are some of the chapter headings:

"Hello, 911, I'm Wedged in This Bank Vault": Clumsy Burglars

"Hi, I'm Butch. I'll Be Your Robber Tonight": Criminal Self-Identification.

"Excuse Me—When's the Next Bus?": The Art of the Getaway

"Officer, That Man Stole My Drugs!": Making It Easy for the Cops.

Laugh we may, just as we may whistle in the dark. But a stupid criminal can pull a trigger, and if the newspaper the next day says it was a "senseless crime," that is cold comfort indeed for the victim. There are pick-pocketing schemes that work like a charm. There are confidence men who can talk intelligent people into parting with their money. There are mobsters who know how to take over major operations. In a word, criminals are dangerous. And what is revealed about evil spirits is sobering. We had better not imagine we can simply outwit them!

Of the few chapters in Swedenborg's *Heaven and Hell* that deal directly with hell, one has the following heading: "The Malice and Heinous Artifices of Infernal Spirits." A new translation by George

---

1. Chuck Shepherd, *America's Least Competent Criminals* (New York: HarperCollins Publishers, 1993.)

Dole makes those heinous artifices "unspeakable skills." Having departed this world, the evil have the advantage over people still living in the world. As Swedenborg puts it, "In the same degree in which angels have wisdom and intelligence, infernal spirits have malice and cunning." There is a malignant craftiness that we could not resist unless protected by God. "This I can testify," says Swedenborg in *Heaven and Hell* 577, "Their malice is so great that it is hardly possible to describe even a thousandth part of it."

An example of devilish cunning occurs in *Arcana Coelestia* 1820, a passage dealing with evil spirits:

> As soon as they detect even the smallest thing that a person loves or get a scent, so to speak, of what is delightful and precious to him, they attack it instantly and try to destroy it, and so the whole person. [They] worm their way into those very loves by flattering them, and in this way they bring a person among themselves. And once they have so brought him in, they very soon try to destroy his loves and so to slay that person, which they do in a thousand unimaginable ways. [If they detect conscience,] they mold an affection out of the falsities and weaknesses that exist with that person, and by means of that affection they dim the light of truth and so pervert it, or else they cause him anxiety and torment. In addition to this, they keep his thought firmly fixed on one single thing; and they fill that thought with delusions, at the same time secretly incorporating evil desire within those delusions. Besides this, they use countless other devices which cannot possibly be described so as to be understood. These are a few of the ways—and

only very general ones—by which they are able to get at a person's conscience.

Another example of devilish cunning and malice has to do with unspeakable menaces toward children.

Swedenborg recorded something in his *Spiritual Diary* that he felt was not suitable for the public to read. It was published in spite of his desire years after his death. He learned about something devilish. It was about "those who had delighted in the filthiest lust of raping infants and small girls." He saw six-year-old girls represented, three years old, even one year old! Although he jotted this down, he wrote with emphasis: *It is not permitted to tell these things publicly, lest they enter into people's thought* (*Spiritual Diary* 2711).

As was stated, this material did not reach the public in Swedenborg's day, but was published after his death. One way the public is reached is through the Internet, and we are witnessing a phenomenon of child pornography that staggers the imagination. First there is the sheer volume of it and its prevalence in so many countries of this world. Scores of thousands of pornographic photos of children are being circulated. And the age of the children! Yes, pornographic photos of little babies! It is hard to believe, and one wishes it were not true. Perhaps this ugly phenomenon is the strongest evidence of a sinister influence from outside this world.

Swedenborg testifies that devils are antagonistic to innocence. "As soon as they see little children they are inflamed with a cruel desire to do them harm" (*Heaven and Hell* 283).

I sometimes puzzle at the paradox that mere fools, such as evils spirits, are so formidable. The better part of valor seems to be to avoid any entanglement or enmeshment with them. There are people who have had harrowing experiences and have offered the warning that devils are a real threat.

A Modern Author Deals with Devils

An insightful writer on spiritual matters, Robert Kirven, wrote the powerful and moving work entitled *A Book about Dying*. This book shows the personal experience of being close to someone at the time of death. Three years previous to its publication, Kirven wrote *Angels in Action*. Although the focus was on angels, he did talk about "evil spirits," and one of his chapters is called "The Battleground." The following is excerpted therefrom.

> The image of good spirits and bad spirits, gathered with conflicting influences around a human spirit who is making some kind of choice—something we humans do, quite a lot of the time— suggests another metaphor. A cliché, popular with political commentators, refers to the president's or Congress' or some political group's waging a battle for the hearts and minds of voters. The two kinds of spirits, those governed by heaven and those governed by hell, do indeed battle for the hearts and minds of human spirits. Because we are spirits clothed in physical bodies, our lives are the battleground.
>
> The apostle Paul wrote that "our struggle is not against enemies of blood and flesh, but against . . . spiritual forces of evil" (Eph.

5:10-17). From that perspective, it could be said that this battle is what life is all about. Our human bodies impel us from the start toward self-preservation, urging us strongly to seek food, clothing, and shelter—whatever we need to stay alive, healthy, and comfortable—without regard for others. Physical survival is self-centered, and this aspect of it can be exploited by evil spirits and turned into selfishness or (given the opportunity) tyranny. As we mature, our human spirit develops other values, loving certain other people, prizing certain things that do not contribute directly to our physical survival, and developing altruistic goals. These are qualities that good spirits encourage and develop into heavenly virtues.[2]

Kirven continues this subject. We offer his practical comments that can find application in real life situations. He says, "the decisions we make, with or against the angels and angelic spirits around us, largely determine our ultimate place in the spiritual world—in heaven or in hell."

This is the circumstance that makes a knowledge of angels and spirits so valuable to us. When we are being tempted, when influences of evil spirits seem attractive or even compelling, some understanding of angels and spirits can help us in a couple of different ways.

For one thing, it can be helpful to know that the attractiveness of something, or the apparent compulsion toward a particular

---

2. Robert H. Kirven, *Angels in Action: What Swedenborg Heard and Saw* (West Chester, Penna.: Chrysalis Books, 1994), 30, 31.

action, can rise out of the influence of evil spirits, rather than out of anything essential or unchangeable in ourselves or in the object of our desire. This knowledge can be power if we use it to objectify our feelings and our rationalizing thoughts, recognizing them as intruders to be repelled. Also, certainty that angels will repel the invading influences for us, if we wholeheartedly seek their help, can free us from the helpless feeling that we must inevitably succumb to the temptation.

Knowing about angels and spirits cannot help us, any more than the angels themselves, if we really want to do what we are tempted to do. Angels can help only those who want help more than anything else, "who are forever striving," as Goethe's angels said about Faust. But if relief from the temptation is what we really want, relief is really there. Really. And it is invincible relief.[3]

Kirven notes that the living experience of temptation by evil spirits never feels as simple as it really is.

Few people really believe the popular but silly excuse for wrongdoing, 'The Devil made me do it!' mostly because so few people believe in the Devil. But the reality of evil spirits, or devils, still gives no credibility to the old excuse, because although devils, or demonic powers, are fearfully real, none can stand before the power of a single angel, an angel who stands always ready if called. Whatever we do, no devil could have made us do it, unless at some level we wanted to do it. If we had unreservedly asked for help, we could have resisted the temptation with help from heaven.

---

3. Ibid., 33.

Our experience of the struggle temptation never appears to be this clear-cut. Many people have discovered that their own Achilles' heel is in the ability to rationalize.

As soon as we start to consider a choice between good and bad actions, or right and wrong motives, we begin to see the infinite shades of gray that really do exist between them and to wonder what we really want, or hope, or believe. Even if we do not begin to ask ourselves these questions, evil spirits always are ready to point them out.[4]

In the final paragraph of this part of his book, Kirven says that the "devil" who tempted Jesus refers "either to one example or the totality of demonic power." It is not a reference to some prince of evil who might, in any sense, be considered an equal opponent of God. He goes on to say, "Accounts of demonic possession of human minds, from the Gospel's healing narratives to the work of Paul Tillich, Rollo May, and M. Scott Peck, are vivid descriptions of terrifying reality. But I have found no depiction of the power of evil that weakens my confidence in the greater power of God and God's angels. If you take seriously the image of life as a battlefield, you will want to be on the side of the angels!"[5]

In that part of the book, Kirven talks of the battleground objectively. One of the features of his book is the inclusion of direct personal experiences. An example follows in which he describes monstrous representations of evil spirits.

As I was falling sleep one night, unwanted fantasies and thoughts

4. Ibid., 34.
5. Ibid., 35.

crowded out what I had been thinking. Feeling too tired and off
guard to resist them, I entertained them as I fell asleep. In a dream,
I climbed steep stairs or a ladder into a dimly lit attic or loft.
Noticing some movement in one corner of the space, I went closer
to investigate. As I approached, a creature climbed down from some
kind of shelf-like perch onto the same level as I was. The thing did
not frighten me so much as it revolted me. It seemed coarse-
skinned, leathery; its arms and legs (or forelegs and hindlegs—it
seemed humanlike, but also inhuman) were about equal in length
and rather long for its body. Its face, also ambiguously human,
displayed beady eyes and big teeth in a mouth spread into a grin or
grimace. The features were close set in a large face.[6]

Kirven felt a loathing for the being he saw, and when he awoke
he was in distress, his heart pounding. He continues:

I had not been asleep long before the dream, and soon fell asleep again
afterwards, more soundly. But as I was dozing off, my horror at this
creature fully occupied my mind, completely crowding out the
unwanted fantasies that had been so persistent before. The next
morning my vivid recollection of the dream led me to realize that the
creature had been a kind of representation of the evil spirits that kept
dragging me into these scenarios and tempting me to enjoy them. Over
time, it or he had grown too strong for me to destroy by my own
strength, and it seemed sure enough of eventual victory that it could
afford to be patient. My feeling, as I thought this, was that the angels

---

6. Ibid., 88.

had warned me about the nature of my adversary by letting me see it. They were guarding me against underestimating the opposition.[7]

Did Kirven regard his situation as unique? On the contrary. He speaks of being held in a state of equilibrium, and says, "In this, I believe I am Everyone, fighting a battle I cannot win alone."

The Antagonism of Devils to Marriage

A chapter in the book *Heaven and Hell* is devoted to the subject of equilibrium between heaven and hell. We who are in between, so to speak, receive influences from both. "From hell there continually breathes forth and ascends an endeavor to do evil, and from heaven there continually breathes forth and descends an endeavor to do good" (*Heaven and Hell* 590). We have mentioned earlier the propensity of evil spirits to stir up fights and to provoke division in human society. A key ingredient in the stability of human society is the institution of marriage.

Swedenborg speaks frequently and emphatically about the sanctity of marriage and of the antagonism of devils towards it. Devils, he says, take delight in destroying that "conjunction of good and truth" which makes heaven. He actually felt an exhalation coming up from hell which opposed love in marriage: "It was like an unceasing endeavor to dissolve and violate marriages" (*Heaven and Hell* 384).

The following are debates and encounters exemplifying a kind of war on marriage.

---

7. Ibid., 89.

Here the question is posed whether marriage differs from adultery.

Once some angels called together several hundred of the cleverest, best-educated, wisest people in all of Europe and asked them about the difference between marriage and adultery, requesting that they consult the reasoning of their own minds. After thinking about it, all but ten of them answered, "Criminal law alone makes the difference. The law exists because it's considered somehow beneficial. We can certainly be aware of this but adapt to it, by exercising caution in public."

They were then asked whether they saw any virtue in marriage or any evil in adultery. "No rational evil or virtue," they answered. Any sin? "Where would that lie? Isn't the deed the same?"

These answers shocked the angels. "Oh, the ignorance today!" they cried out. "How terrible and how immense it is!"

The companies of the wise turned around when they heard this and roared with laughter among themselves. "Ignorance!" they said. "Can any wisdom serve to convince that loving another man's wife merits eternal damnation?"

Marriage Love 478:2

A devil makes his case in favor of adultery.

"As everyone knows, the pleasure afforded by adultery is far superior to the pleasure given by marriage. Adulterers are always on fire, and so they live a faster-paced, busier, more active life than those who live with just one woman. Love with your married partner, on the other hand, grows cool. Sometimes it gets so cold that hardly a single word or moment of intimacy remains alive between you.

"It's different with whores. Life with your wife is deadening, because you lose you ability to perform, but extramarital sex restores and revitalizes you. Isn't it in sleeping with a number of women that you find renewal and reinvigoration in place of deadly boredom?

"What *is* marriage but legal whoredom? Who can tell the difference? Can love be forced? And yet love with your wife is forced by contract and by law. Isn't love with your married partner the same as sexual desire? And this is so universal that even birds and beasts have it. What is married love but sexual desire? And you can feel desire for *any* woman.

"We have laws against adultery because the people who passed the laws believed that it was for the common good. But the lawmakers and judges themselves are capable of sleeping around and saying to each other, 'Let those who are without sin cast the first stone.'

"Only simpletons and religious fanatics believe that adultery is a sin; not the intelligent. Like us they see the matter in Nature's light. Doesn't adultery result in offspring as often as marriage does? Aren't illegitimate children just as capable and useful in employment and service as the legitimate ones? Besides, it provides a solution for families that would otherwise be childless. Isn't that beneficial rather than harmful?

"What does it hurt a wife to take on a number of rivals? What does it hurt a man to have this stain on his reputation? It's only a silly prejudice based on a delusion.

"The reason the church has laws and regulations against adultery is for the sake of hierarchical power, but what do theology and spirituality have to do with a pleasure merely of the body and the flesh? Aren't there elders and monks who act this way? And does it stop them from acknowledging and worshiping God?"

Marriage Love 500:2,3

A military officer has no qualms about adultery.

There were certain spirits who, out of a habit developed in bodily life, were harassing me with special skill. They entered in a fairly gentle stream, moving somewhat like a wave. It is usually honest spirits who enter this way, but I could tell that various ruses and similar devices for ensnaring and deceiving others were involved.

Eventually, I spoke with one of the spirits. He told me that he had been an army general when he was alive in the world. Since I detected something lecherous in his thoughts, I talked to him about marriage. (When spirits speak, visible pictures representing their thoughts appear, giving those ideas full and very rapid expression.)

He said that in the life of the body he had not felt adultery counted for anything. "Adultery is unutterably wicked," I was permitted to reply, "even though people like you are persuaded by the pleasure you've felt in it that it's not and in fact is perfectly legitimate.

"You could have recognized its true nature from the fact that marriages are the breeding grounds for the human race and in consequence for the heavenly kingdom. This consideration should indicate that marriage ought never to be violated but rather to be held sacred.

"You could also have recognized it because you ought to know, now that you're in the next life where you can perceive it, that the love in marriage comes down through heaven from the Lord. You should be able to see that married love gives birth to mutual love, the foundation of heaven.

"Yet another indication should have been that as soon as adulterers draw near any community in heaven they become aware of their own stench and hurl themselves down from there towards hell.

"At the very least, you could have realized that violating marriage is against divine law, against civil law everywhere, and against the genuine light of reason, because it goes against order, both divine and human; not to mention other considerations."

But he answered that he had known nothing of the kind during his earthly life and had never even given it any thought. He wanted to debate the validity of my statements, but I said, "Truth is not a topic for debate in the next world because arguments tend to provide a defense for pleasure and so for evil and falsity.

"First, you ought to think about the things I said, because they're true. Or you ought to base your thinking on the following principle, which is very well known in the world: we should not do to others what we don't want them to do to us. If anyone had seduced your wife, whom you once loved (as everyone does in the beginning of marriage), you'd have been in a fury over it. Surely you yourself, speaking under the influence of that rage, would have reviled adultery as well. And since you're gifted, wouldn't you have come up with even more arguments against it than anyone else? Wouldn't you in fact have damned it to hell? So you could have judged from your own experience."

Arcana Coelestia 2733

Swedenborg listens to a private conversation.

Certain satyrs were talking about marriage, nature, and religion.

Marriage was taken up by the satyrs who looked as though they had calves' feet. "What is marriage but legal adultery?" they said. "What could be sweeter than pretending virtue while practicing vice? Or sneaking around behind a husband's back?"

The others chortled and applauded.

Nature was the subject of the satyrs who appeared to have panther feet. "What is there besides nature?" they said. "What distinction exists between human beings and animals except the fact that people can use words to communicate while animals use sounds? Doesn't nature work to provide both of them with life (by means of heat) and intelligence (by means of light)?"

"Hey, you sure know what you're talking about!" shouted all the others.

Religion was addressed by the satyrs who seemed to have the feet of wolves. "What is God, or the Divinity, if not nature operating at its deepest level? What is religion but an invention designed to seize and shackle the mass of humankind?"

"Bravo!" cheered the rest.

Moments later the crowd broke up. As they scattered, they saw me staring at them from a distance. Irritated, they dashed out of the woods where they had been meeting and hurried toward me with menacing glares. "Why are you standing here listening to our private whispers?" they demanded.

"Why not?" I answered. "What's to stop me? You were talking out loud." And I reported what I had heard them say.

This cooled their vehemence, since they were afraid that what they had said would get out. They began to speak modestly and act with decorum, which told me that they were not from the lower classes but well-born. . . .

I asked them whether they had ever thought of adultery as a sin. "Sin?" they answered. "We don't know what that is."

"Do you have any memory of hearing that adultery goes against the sixth of the ten commandments?" I asked.

"The ten commandments! What are they?" they answered. "Isn't that a religious primer? What do men like us have to do with a childish little rule book like that?"

"Have you ever given any thought to hell?"

"Who's come up out of hell to tell us about it?"

"While you were in the world, did you ever think about life after death?"

"It's the same as for animals," they said. "Or maybe the same as for ghosts. If ghosts do waft up out of the corpse, they dissolve."

"Did the priests never tell you about any of this?" I probed.

"We just listened to the sound of their voices," they replied. "We didn't pay any attention to what they said or what it meant."

parts of *Marriage Love* 521:2,3,5

We see the plight of a man who boasted of sexual conquests.

I once listened to a spirit newly arrived from the world—a young man—bragging about his sexual exploits. He was trying to earn a reputation as a man more masculine than others. Amid all his swaggering, he gave vent to the following.

"What could be gloomier than imprisoning your love and living one man with one woman? What could be happier than liberating your love? We all find our energy sapped by sticking with one woman and find it renewed by having lots of them, don't we?

"What could be sweeter than unhampered promiscuity? Than a constant succession of partners? Girls to rob of their virginity? Husbands to fool? A halo to wear while sleeping around? Everyone knows that the things we obtain by trickery, deceit, and stealth bring the deepest pleasure to our minds."

"Don't talk that way," said his listeners. "You don't know where you are or who the people around you are. You've just gotten here.

"Under your feet is hell and over your head is heaven. You're presently in a region called the world of spirits, midway between those two. This is where everyone departing the world arrives and is brought together for an investigation of character. Here the evil prepare for hell and the good for heaven.

"Maybe you remember hearing priests in the world say that

people who sleep around and people who engage in prostitution go down to hell and that faithful married partners go up to heaven."

That made the newcomer laugh. "What's heaven?" he said. "What's hell? Isn't heaven a place where everyone is free? And those who get to love as many as they wish are free. Isn't hell a place where everyone is enslaved? And those who are obligated to stick to one partner are slaves."

But a certain angel looking down from heaven heard what he said and interrupted, to keep him from going so far as to profane marriage. "Come up here," he told the spirit. "I'll let you see personally what heaven and hell are, and what hell is like for those who've justified a life devoid of sexual morals."

After welcoming the spirit, he led him into a garden of paradise. The garden contained fruit trees and flowers that by their beauty, charm, and fragrance filled the observer's breast with pleasure in being alive. The spirit viewing them was struck with great admiration. But he was then looking at them with his external vision, the same power of sight he had used on their counterparts in the world. In looking at things this way, he was rational.

When it came to perceiving internally, though, free sex took the lead and occupied every split second of his thinking. In looking at things on this level, he was not rational. As a consequence, his external vision was closed off, and his inner vision opened up.

"What am I looking at now?" he said, once his inner eyes opened. "Isn't this a bunch of dead straw and wood? What am I

picking up now—some foul odor? Where did the beauties of
paradise go?"

"They're present right close by," said the angel. "But they're not
visible to your inner eyes, which see through the lens of illicit sex.
This lens turns everything of heaven into something hellish. It
keeps you from seeing anything but the opposite of what's there.

"Each one of us has an inner mind and an outer mind, so we
have an inner way of seeing and an outer way. For those who are
evil, the inner mind is crazy and the outer mind sane. But for those
who are good, the inner mind is sane and allows the outer mind to
be so as well. The character of the mind determines how the
person views objects in the spiritual world."

Next, the angel used a power given him to close off the spirit's
inner vision and open his outer vision, and led him through some
gates toward the heart of the residential area. There the spirit saw
magnificent palaces made of alabaster, marble, and different kinds
of precious stone. They had porticos attached to them and pillars
all around with stunning embellishments and ornamentation
covering and twining about them.

The spirit stood astounded at the sight. "What am I looking
at?" he said. "I'm looking at marvels in their true magnificence.
I'm looking at feats of architecture in their true artistry."

But then the angel again closed off his outer way of seeing and
opened up the inner way, which was a bad one, since it was
distorted by flagrant promiscuity. "What am I seeing now?" he
cried out. "Where am I? What happened to the magnificent
palaces? All I can see are heaps of rubble and empty caverns."

His external sight soon restored, he was taken into one of the palaces, where he saw adornment on doorways, windows, walls, and ceilings, and most of all on the furnishings, which were decorated all over with heavenly designs worked in gold and precious stone. There is no language to describe them and no art to depict them; they surpass the ideas expressed in words and the conceptions expressed in art. On seeing them the spirit again cried out, "These are absolute wonders, which no eye has ever seen!"

But then his inner sight was opened up, his outer was shut down as before, and he was asked, "What do you see now?"

"Nothing but fences of reed here, straw there, and kindling in another place," he answered.

Once more, though, he was restored to his superficial state of mind, and young women were ushered in—lovely girls, because they embodied heavenly feelings. In a voice ringing sweetly with affection. they addressed him.

Then did the sights he was seeing and the sounds he was hearing bring a change over his face, and spontaneously he reverted to his deeper, obscene nature. Because obscenity cannot bear anything of heavenly love in the least, and because heavenly love in turn cannot bear obscenity either, they vanished to each other's sight—the young women from the man and the man from the young women.

Later, the angel explained to him the reason for the conversions of the objects he saw. "I can tell," he said, "that in the world from which you've arrived you were two-faced—one thing on the inside and another on the outside. On the surface, you were a law-abiding, ethical, and rational human being. Internally, however, you were not law-abiding, ethical, or rational, because you were a devotee of promiscuity and an adulterer. People of that kind, when they're allowed to go up into heaven, are able to see heavenly sights there as long as they keep up their facade. When their deeper nature comes out, though, they see hellish things instead of the heavenly ones.

"But you should know that, for every person here, external characteristics are gradually closed off and the internal ones are brought out. That's how people are prepared for heaven or hell. Since the evil of dedicated promiscuity more than any other pollutes the deeper parts of the mind, you can't help being dragged down to the level of the filth you love. That filth is in hell, with its caverns that reek of excrement.

"Is there anyone who can't use reason to see that, in the spiritual world, anything unchaste or lewd is impure and unclean? Obviously, nothing defiles and pollutes a person more or introduces more of hell into him.

"Be careful, then, not to revel in your obscenities any longer, bragging that they make you a man more masculine than others. I'm telling you you'll end up such a weakling that you'll hardly know where your masculinity is. That's what happens to people who preen themselves on their sexual prowess."

The spirit went back down to the world of spirits and returned to his former companions, speaking modestly and chastely to them. But not for long.

Marriage Love 477

Indifference and contempt are expressed on the question of the sacred and marriage.

The same angel who had been my guide and companion in visits to ancients of the four previous ages—Golden, Silver, Copper, and Iron—returned once again. "Do you want to see the era that followed those ancient ones?" he asked. "Do you want to see what it was and still is like? Follow me. . . ."

We had made it through a terrifying forest and now started into a desert no less daunting. It consisted of piles of stone interspersed with ditches that had water snakes and vipers crawling out of them and flying serpents taking flight. The whole desert was one long, downward slope.

We continued down this extended incline until we arrived in a valley inhabited by the people of that region and era. There were huts here and there, which finally came together in the semblance of a town. We entered and discovered that the houses were built of charred tree branches stuck together with mud, the roofs being black shingle. The streets were crooked, narrow at the head but widening as they went until they were downright spacious where they ended in public squares. (There were, consequently, as many squares as there were streets.)

As we entered the town, the sky was swallowed up in darkness, so we looked up, received some light, and were able to see. I asked whatever spirits I came across, "Can you see? Because the sky doesn't show above you."

"What are you talking about?" they answered. "We can see clearly. We're walking in broad daylight!"

"Darkness is light to them," the angel told me, "and light is darkness, just as it is to a nocturnal bird, since they look down and not up."

We entered dwellings here and there. In each, we saw a man with his woman. "Do you all live here in your own houses with just the one wife?" we asked.

"What do you mean, 'just the one wife'?" they hissed. "Why not ask whether we live with just the one whore? What's a wife but a whore?

"Our laws don't let us shack up with more than just the one female. Still, it's not a scandal or disgrace for us to sleep with more of them, we just have to keep it outside the house. We brag to each other about it. This way we enjoy more license and end up with greater carnal pleasure than polygamists.

"Why aren't we allowed to take a number of wives when all the lands around us were given the privilege and still have it today? What's life with just one woman but bondage and imprisonment? But we in this place have shattered the jail's lock, rescued ourselves from slavery, and set ourselves free. How could anyone be angry with the prisoner who liberates himself when he can?"

"Friend," we answered, "you talk as if you're devoid of religion. What individual with a modicum of reason doesn't know that adultery is profane and hellish or that marriage is sacred and heavenly? Isn't adultery the province of devils in hell and marriage the province of angels in heaven? You must have read the sixth commandment, and the passage in which Paul says that adulterers can in no way enter heaven."

Our host guffawed at this and looked at me as if I was an idiot and nearly insane.

But at that exact moment a messenger from the mayor of the town ran up. "Lead the two newcomers to the public square," he said. "If they're reluctant, drag them there. We saw them in a fog of light; they entered secretly; they're spies."

"We seemed to be in a fog," the angel told me, "because to them the heavenly light that surrounded us is shadowy while the shadows of hell are light. They see it backwards because they count sin—even adultery—as nothing and therefore completely mistake falsity for truth. Falsity shines brightly for the satans in hell, and truth darkens their vision just as much as the shades of night do."

"You don't have to talk us into going to the forum, much less drag us there," we said to the messenger. "We'll go with you willingly." And off we went.

There we saw a large crowd, and several legal experts who moved away from it to whisper in our ear. "Be careful," they said. "Don't say anything against religion, the form of government, or good morals."

"We won't speak except in support of those things and in the interest of them," we answered.

"What does your religion teach about marriage?" we asked.

The crowd muttered at this. "Why concern yourselves with marriage here?" they said. "Marriage is marriage."

"What does your religion teach about promiscuity?" we asked next.

The crowd muttered at this too. "Why concern yourselves with promiscuity here?" they said. "Sleeping around is sleeping around. Let one who is without sin cast the first stone."

"Does your religion teach that marriage is sacred and heavenly and that adultery is profane and hellish?" was our third question.

At this, many in the crowd cackled, smirked, and jeered. "Ask our priests about religious subjects," they said, "not us. We yield to absolutely everything they say, because religion doesn't even begin to come under the intellect's scrutiny. Haven't you heard that the mind goes crazy when it worries about the mysteries that are the sum and substance of religion?

"And how do the things we do have any bearing on religion? Isn't it the pious murmurings of the heart about expiation, satisfaction, and imputation that beatify the soul, and not works?"

But now some of the "wiser" citizens approached. "Remove yourselves from here," they said. "The crowd is getting angry. Pretty soon there'll be a riot. Let's discuss this subject by ourselves. There's a footpath behind city hall; let's go there. Come with us." We followed.

Then they asked us, "Where are you from? And what's your business here?"

"To learn about marriage," we said. "It was a holy rite for the ancient peoples who lived in the Golden, Silver, and Copper Ages, and we want to know whether it's so for you too or not."

"What do you mean 'holy rite,'" they replied. "Isn't it the work of the flesh and of the night?"

"Isn't it also the work of the spirit?" we answered. "And what the flesh does at the behest of the spirit, isn't that spiritual? Everything the spirit does, it does from the union of goodness and truth. Isn't that the spiritual marriage that enters into the natural marriage of husband and wife?"

"You're making the whole thing too refined and subtle," those so-called wise men responded. "You're climbing up above sound reason to spiritual levels. How can anyone start up there and come down to judge well of any matter?

"Perhaps you have eagles' wings," they added mockingly. "Maybe you can soar up to the top of heaven and see right through such things. We can't."

"Tell us, from the lofty region where the winged ideas of your minds do fly," we requested, "whether you can and do grasp these facts: There is such a thing as married love between one man and one wife. That love gathers into itself all the blessings, happiness, joy, sweetness, and pleasures of heaven. It comes from the Lord and depends on people's acceptance of good and truth from him, and so on the state of their religious development."

The "sages" turned their backs. "These men are out of their minds," they said. "They're going up where the air is thin to judge of affairs. They're just scattering trifles when they spout these meaningless oracles."

Then they turned back to us. "We'll make direct replies to your windy fortune-telling and dreams," they said. "What does married love have in common with religion or with inspiration from God?

"The existence of that love with each of us, of course, depends on our ability to perform in bed. Doesn't that ability exist in gentiles just as much as Christians? And in the sacrilegious as much as the religious? Everyone knows that the potency of love comes from heredity or health or clean living or a warm climate, and that it can be strengthened and aroused by certain potions.

"Don't animals have it too? Especially birds that mate in love, pair by pair.

"That love belongs to the flesh, doesn't it? What does the flesh have in common with the spiritual state of the church? Is there the least bit of difference in the physical expression of that love with your wife from what it is with a prostitute? Isn't the libido the same, and the pleasure too? So it's wrongful to trace the origin of married love back to the holy things of the church."

"You're arguing at the goading of lust," we said to them, "not out of a love for marriage. You have no idea at all what married love is because it's cold in you.

"Your words prove to us that you belong to the age named for its origin and essence as an age of iron and clay, which fail to stick together, as Daniel prophesied in chapter, 2, verse 43. You're making marital love and obscene love into one thing. Can they stick together any better than iron and clay? You believe in your wisdom and people call you wise, but if there's one thing you're not, it's wise."

Burning with anger, they raised a shout and called on the crowd to throw us out. But we, with a power the Lord gave us, stretched out our hands, and there in the sight of all were the creeping things of the desert—the flying serpents, vipers, and water snakes, and dragons as well. They invaded the town and filled it up, driving the inhabitants away in terror.

"Newcomers from earth reach this place daily, and their predecessors in turn are sent off and plummet into gorges in the west," the angel told me. "From a distance these chasms look like lakes of fire and brimstone. Everyone there is an adulterer in both spirit and body."

Marriage Love 79

V

Madness and Evil Spirits

The presence of devils or evil spirits is not something of which a person is normally conscious. (Nor indeed is the presence of angels evident.) But what about certain people who have severe mental difficulties? A clinical psychiatrist who worked with mental patients for more than a dozen years made what he considered a break through discovery in 1964. His findings may be found in a book called *The Presence of Other Worlds*.

Wilson Van Dusen came to accept the concept of an interaction of human minds with a hierarchy of spirits. "This interaction is normally not conscious, but perhaps in some cases of mental illness it has become conscious."[1] This statement and the things

---

1. Wilson Van Dusen, *The Presence of Other Worlds: The Psychological /Spiritual Finds of Emanuel Swedenborg* (1974; rpt. West Chester, Penna.: Chrysalis Books, 1991), 161.

that now follow are taken from a chapter devoted to this point in the book just mentioned.

> At best our patients would tell us a few striking hallucinations. [This took place at the Mendocina State Hospital in Ukiah, California.] An unusually cooperative patient led me to ask if I could talk directly with her hallucinations. I did, and she gave me their immediate response. I had stumbled upon a way to get a much richer picture of the inner world of hallucinations.

He began to look for patients who could distinguish between their own thoughts and the things they were hearing or seeing. He would work with a patient for as little as one hour or as long as several months of inquiry. He reported that he found great consistency in what was reported independently by different patients. One consistent finding was that patients felt they had contact with another world or order of beings. All objected to the term "hallucination" but preferred to coin their own terms.

> In my dialogues with patients I learned of two orders of experience, borrowing from the voices themselves, called the higher and the lower order. Lower-order voices are similar to drunken bums at a bar who like to tease and torment just for the fun of it. They suggest lewd acts and then scold the patient for considering them. They find a weak point of conscience and work on it interminably.[2]

---

2. Ibid., 162.

We can imagine how intrigued Dr. Van Dusen was with some of the things he discovered in Swedenborg's works. Take, for example, this statement about diabolical spirits, found in *Arcana Coelestia* 1917: "It is common with them to induce a falsity from themselves, and then at the same time to make it the subject of accusation." Swedenborg reports that spirits keep a person's thoughts firmly fixed on one single thing, "and they fill that thought with delusions, at the same time secretly incorporating evil desires within those delusions" (*Arcana Coelestia* 1820).

Getting back to Van Dusen's findings, he describes at length the malicious nature of the voices that trouble patients. "They invade every nook and cranny of privacy, work on every weakness and belief, claim awesome powers, lie, make promises, and then undermine the patient's will." He says that their voice quality can change or shift, leaving the patient confused:

> A few ideas can be repeated endlessly. One voice just said "hey" for months while the patient tried to figure out whether "hey" or "hay" was meant. All of the lower order are irreligious or antireligious. In one case they appeared to the patient as conventional devils and referred to themselves as demons. In a few instances they referred to themselves as from hell.[3]

Those of the "higher order" seem to have an angelic quality. In quantity, they make up "perhaps a fifth or less of the patients'

---

3. Ibid., 163.

experiences." Says Van Dusen, "Some patients experience both the higher and lower orders at various times and feel caught between a private heaven and hell. Many only know the attacks of the lower order." Although the higher order seems to have power over the lower, it is "not enough to give peace of mind to most patients."

> Some people might suspect that my manner of questioning fed back to the patients what I wanted to hear, but I had occasion to address an audience of patients and staff in the hospital on hallucinations. Afterward many patients I had not met came up and pressed my hand and said I had described their experiences too. As incredible as it may seem, I'm inclined to believe, the above is a roughly accurate account of many patients' hallucinatory experiences.[4]

In *Heaven and Hell* 248–249, Swedenborg states the following:

> The speech of an angel or spirit with man is heard as sonorously as the speech of a person with a person, yet not by others who stand near, but by himself alone. The reason is that the speech of an angel or spirit flows first into a person's thought and by an internal way into his organ of hearing thus affecting from within . . . to speak with spirits is rarely granted at this day, because it is dangerous; for then the spirits know, what otherwise they do not know, that they are with people, and evil spirits are such they regard people with deadly hatred, and desire nothing more than to destroy them, both soul and body. This in fact is done with those who have indulged

---

4. Ibid., 164.

much in fantasies . . . Some also who lead a solitary life occasionally hear spirits talking with them.

Van Dusen ponders the statement that, if evil spirits knew they were with people, they would do all sorts of things to torment them and destroy their life, commenting that it is not clear how the barrier between spirits and humans is penetrated. He does not recommend a credulous attempt to learn from spirits. On the contrary, he quotes the following from Swedenborg's *Spiritual Experiences* 1622:

> When spirits begin to speak with man, he must beware lest he believe them in anything; for they say almost anything; things are fabricated by them, and they lie; for if they were permitted to relate what heaven is, and how things are in the heavens they would tell so many lies, and indeed with a solemn affirmation, that one would be astonished. . . . They are extremely fond of fabricating: and whenever any subject of discourse is proposed, they think that they know it, and give their opinions one after another, one in one way, and another in another, altogether as if they know; and if one listens and believes, they press on, and deceive, and seduce in divers ways.

In Van Dusen's treatment of this subject, he will admit, "I am guessing at this point." And in concluding this chapter, he says the following:

> My guess is that Swedenborg systematically explored the same worlds that psychotic patients find themselves thrust into, and

these worlds are heaven and hell, the worlds beyond this one, inside this one. It is not too surprising, when you think of it, that persons who are disordered inwardly experience some of the raw underpinnings of experience that are invisible to the smoothly functioning mind. . . . The only thing left that is really yours is the struggle to choose. Those who aren't choosing are going the way the spiritual winds blow. So the pitiful picture of the hallucinated psychotic is really an exaggerated picture of everyone's situation.[5]

Our Own Demonic Thoughts

From time to time, we entertain unusual thoughts, and they may not seem so crazy when we are into them. The value in reading what devils think can give us an objective view of some typical human thoughts when taken to their extreme.

The following from *Arcana Coelestia* 7217 provides an extreme example of negative human thinking:

> What are faith and charity? Are they not mere words? And what is conscience? Feeling distressed on account of these things is feeling distressed over nothing . . . What wealth and prominence are we can see with our eyes, and we feel with pleasure that they really exist, for they swell the body and fill it with joy.

When it comes to the motivation for doing anything worth-

---

5. Ibid., 165.

while, what is the thought of a devil's heart? *Heaven and Hell* 555 puts it this way:

> Who has ever done any worthwhile, useful, and distinguished deed except for the sake of being praised and honored by others, or regarded with esteem and honor by others? And can this be from any other source than the fire of love for glory and honor, consequently for self?

Contemplating a useful deed, one might find oneself saying inwardly, "How does it concern me? Why should I? What's in it for me?" There are debates within our own minds, and that is one reason it can help to be a spectator of debates in the spiritual world. The following is a collection of such debates.

Swedenborg challenges people who complained that they had not been sufficiently warned.

I have heard many people newly arrived from the world complaining that they did not know the final outcome of their life would depend on what they loved. They said that, while they were in the world, they did not think about their preferences, still less about their pleasures, because whatever pleased them they loved. They believed that a person's fate depended simply on intelligent thinking—especially when such thinking was the result of piety and of faith.

But I answered that, if they had wanted to, they could have known that an evil life is not pleasing to heaven or delightful to God but is pleasing to hell and delightful to the devil. They could have known, on the other hand, that a good life is pleasing to heaven and delightful to God, while it is not pleasing to hell or delightful to the devil. From this, they could have figured out that it is the nature of evil to stink and of good to smell fragrant.

Since they could have known this if they had wanted, I went on, why hadn't they fled evil as hellish and diabolical? Why had they indulged in it just because it pleased them? And because they now knew that the enjoyment of evil reeked so badly, they should also have realized that no one brimming with those smells could make it into heaven.

At this response, they took off to join others whose pleasures matched their own, because only there among their like and nowhere else could they breathe.

Divine Providence 305

Spirits cannot believe it when Swedenborg tells them when life really begins.

I once spoke with people in the next life who were attached to the pleasures of evil and falsity. "You won't be really living," I was given to say to them, "until you've been deprived of your pleasures."

But they said, just as people like them in the world do, "If we were deprived of our pleasures, then we'd no longer have any life at all."

"But that's the point at which life first begins," I was allowed to answer, "and along with it the kind of happiness they have in heaven—a happiness so far beyond yours that it cannot be described."

This they could not grasp, because whatever is unfamiliar seems unreal. The same thing happens with people in the world. Everyone there who is under the sway of self-love and love of worldly things, everyone who is consequently devoid of charity, is well-acquainted with the joy of the first two loves but not with that of the last one—charity. As a result, they have absolutely no idea what charity is, still less that a person could find any joy in charity.

In reality, the joy of charity is what fills the whole of heaven and produces the blessedness and happiness there. It even produces the intelligence and wisdom there, if you will believe it, with all their attendant pleasures. It is the joy of charity that the Lord flows into, bringing the bright light of truth and the warm flame of goodness and, consequently, bringing intelligence and wisdom. But falsity and evil reject those qualities. They suffocate and pervert them, producing stupidity and madness.

All this clarifies which of the joys connected with our affections answers to the happiness of eternal life and what the quality of that joy is.

Arcana Coelestia 3938:5

A church official failed to see a difference between the heavenly and the infernal.

Very few people these days know anything about spiritual good or about freedom either, as I learned by experience from people coming from the Christian world into the next life. Let me introduce just one example to illustrate.

There was a certain highly placed church official who considered himself better educated than others and was acknowledged during his lifetime to be a well-educated man. Because he had lived an evil life, he labored under such brainless ignorance about goodness and freedom, and about the joy and blessings resulting from them, that he was unaware of the slightest difference between the joy and freedom in hell and the joy and freedom in heaven. As a matter of fact, he said no difference existed.

Arcana Coelestia 4136:3

Spirits who had never bothered with the needs of others exemplify hellish love.

The joy that flows out of self-love completely chokes off the joy that comes from heavenly love, so much so that it leaves people without the slightest awareness of what heavenly joy is. If any description of heavenly joy is given to them, they meet it with disbelief and even denial.

I had the opportunity to learn this from some evil spirits in the next life—ones who, during their life in the world, had failed to help their neighbor or their native land in any way unless it benefitted themselves. These spirits discount the possibility of finding joy in good deeds unless reward is an incentive. When the hope of reward is gone, they believe, all joy ceases.

You can tell them that the moment such joy ceases heavenly joy begins, but they react with mute amazement. Their astonishment increases when they hear that this heavenly joy enters by way of our inmost depths and touches our hearts and minds with happiness beyond description. At this, they are thunderstruck and say they cannot comprehend it. In fact, they admit they do not want to. They believe that, if they give up the joy of self-love, they will be miserable because none of life's joy will remain. Anyone with a different frame of mind they call naive.

Not much different are those who do perform good but with a

view to reward. The good they do is for their own benefit rather than for others, because they are looking out for themselves in what they do. They pay no regard to their fellow human beings, their country, heaven, or the Lord except as debtors owing them a favor.

Arcana Coelestia 6391:2, 3

A dreadful sensation was experienced by people who wanted to be instantaneously transformed.

There were certain people who, while in the world, believed in instantaneous salvation gained directly through mercy. When they became spirits, they wanted God in his omnipotence and at the same time in his mercy to transform the hellish delight they felt in doing evil into the heavenly pleasure of doing good. As this was what they craved, some angels received permission to bring it about and took away their hellish pleasure. But because that pleasure came from what they loved most in life, so that it was life itself for them, they now lay as dead, bereft of all sensation and motion. No kind of life could be breathed into them, either, except their own.

The reason was that every part of their mind and body had been turned backwards and could not be wrenched around to face the opposite direction. As a result, they were revived by having the enjoyment of their favorite thing in life returned to them. Afterward, they said that during the coma they had felt a dreadful sensation, somehow horrifying, which they refused to talk about.

All this explains why they say in heaven that it is easier to change an owl into a turtledove or a snake into a lamb than to turn a spirit from hell into one of heaven's angels.

Divine Providence 338:7

An experiment showed punishment and fear cannot change people.

I witnessed just how far they were able [to resist evil] when they heard about the punishments in hell, in fact, saw and also felt them, all to no effect. They steeled their minds, saying, "This can happen and that can occur as long as I have my heart's gratifications and joy while I'm here. I know what I'm facing right now, I don't think about what's to come. Nothing worse happens to me than to many, many others."

But when the time comes, they find themselves thrust into hell, where punishments force them to stop doing wrong. Still, the punishment does not rob them of the will, the intention, or the resulting thought to do evil. It only puts an end to the acts.

Apocalypse Explained 1165

VI
The Conquest of Devils in the Ministry of Christ

We mentioned at the beginning of this book that Jesus was attacked by evil spirits and that a vital part of his ministry was to cast them out. The first miracle recorded in the Gospel of Mark is the casting out of an evil spirit. Once, as noted already, Jesus asked the name of an evil spirit, to which the reply was, "My name is Legion, for we are many."

According to the Gospel of John, Jesus began the public part of his ministry with a startling act and dramatic pronouncement, which no one at that time understood. He cast out of the temple the corrupt money changers who had taken it over. "My house shall be called a house of prayer for all nations but you have made it a den of thieves."What was the significance, what was the real meaning of this act of casting out? Witnesses there demanded some sign, some explanation, and Jesus replied, "Destroy this temple, and in three days I will raise it up." What an amazing thing to say! It is evident that people did not grasp the real meaning of it. "It has taken forty-six years to build that temple, and will you raise it up in three days?" (John 2:21).

According to the synoptic gospels, this same act of casting out took place again at the end of Jesus' ministry. Yes, he was speaking of the temple of his body. And as the work of the ministry was coming to its climax he said, "Now is the judgment of this world; now the ruler of this world will be cast out" (John 12:31). As the work of Jesus progressed, seventy of his disciples came to him exclaiming with joy, "Lord, even the demons are subject to us in your name," and he said to them, "I saw Satan fall like lightning from heaven." (Do you remember that this was the verse St. Jerome took to refer to what he named "Lucifer"?) Jesus then told them that he was giving them authority "over all the power of the enemy" (Luke 10:17-19).

"He was speaking of the temple of his body." According to Swedenborg, Jesus came to make himself vulnerable, to allow the forces of hell that were attacking others to attack him. And if they were cast out of the temple of his being, this would have most significant consequences for the peace of the human mind. The human mind is ideally a house in which God may be freely worshiped. "My house is a house of prayer." According to

Swedenborg, Jesus restored peace and freedom to the house of the human mind.

The gospel phenomenon of casting out devils is one thing. But Swedenborg says that the work of redemption from evil spirits is portrayed also in other acts. Consider the calming of the storm upon the sea: "Then he arose and rebuked the wind, and said to the sea, 'Peace, be still!' And the wind ceased and there was a great calm" (Mark 4:39). Swedenborg says that the words here were "as if he were speaking to those things or those persons that induce temptations." For the incident of a miracle involves more than the safety of a handful of men on a certain day in history. Swedenborg says the miracle "involves arcana of heaven and interior things, . . . spiritual temptations" (*Apocalypse Explained* 419:24). The exhibition of power against the sea is dramatic enough, but Swedenborg says, "By a like divine power the Lord fights at this day against hell in every person who is being regenerated." This is from the work *True Christian Religion* in the chapter on redemption, where Swedenborg asserts that the work of Jesus in redeeming mankind through overcoming evil spirits was a work of infinite power. The assertion is that he fought and does fight for us in what are called "temptations":

> Redemption was a purely Divine work. He who knows what hell is, and to what height it had risen and how it had overflowed the whole world of spirits at the time of the Lord's coming, and with what might the Lord cast it down and scattered it, and afterwards brought into order both hell and heaven, cannot but wonder and declare that all this must have been a purely Divine work. First, as

to the nature of hell. It consists of myriads of myriads, since it consists of all those who from the creation of the world have alienated themselves from God by evils of life and falsities of belief. . . . By a like Divine power the Lord fights at this day.

True Christian Religion 123

Temptations

In human "temptations" as described by Swedenborg, there is no awareness of the presence of evil spirits. There is only an awareness of anxiety and mental anguish: "Spiritual temptations are pains of mind induced by evil spirits" (*Heavenly Doctrines* 187). Someone undergoing temptation is aware of being ill at ease or having a greater or lesser degree of anxiety. Sometimes there is a relentless "drawing forth, and bringing to remembrance of the evil which one has committed":

> The person does not know that such assaults are from evil spirits, because he does not know that spirits are present with him, evil spirits in his evils, and good spirits in his goods; and that they are in his thoughts and affections. These temptations are most grievous when they are accompanied with bodily pains; and still more so, when those pains are of long continuance.

Heavenly Doctrines 196

The painful memory syndrome is described in *Arcana Coelestia* 741 as follows:

Temptations are nothing other than conflicts between evil spirits and angels who reside with a person. Evil spirits activate all the dishonorable things the person had done or even thought which have been with him since early childhood, thus both evils and falsities; and in so doing, the spirits condemn him, for nothing gives them greater delight. Indeed the very delight of their life consists in doing just that. But the Lord protects the person by means of angels and prevents the evil spirits and demons from overstepping the mark and overwhelming him with more than he can cope with.

A few paragraphs later, in *Arcana Coelestia* 751, we read that those who are in temptation

are not aware of anything other than the feeling that it is something within them which is suffering in this way. . . . There are evil spirits who at that time activate a person's falsities and evils, as has been stated. Indeed they draw out of his memory whatever he has thought and carried out since early childhood. Evil spirits do this so cleverly and wickedly as to defy description. But the angels who are with him draw out his goods and truths, and in this way defend him. This conflict is what the person feels and perceives in himself and is what causes the sting and torment of conscience.

The Lord's fighting for people against evil spirits Swedenborg sees represented in the battles described in the Old Testament, especially in passages in the prophets, such as Isaiah 63, which speaks of the "redeeming" work of the Lord. He trod the winepress alone and his arm brought salvation. "So he became their savior. In all their affliction he was afflicted, and the angel of his presence saved them; In his love and in his pity he redeemed them; and he bore them and carried them all the days of old" (Isaiah 63:8–9).

The following example typifies Swedenborg's teaching on the temptations of Jesus:

> The Lord's life in the world from earliest childhood consisted in constant temptation and constant victory. The last was when on the Cross he prayed for his enemies, and so for all people in the whole world. In the part of the Word where the Lord's life is described—in the Gospels—no other temptation, apart from the last, is mentioned than his temptation in the wilderness. More than this was not disclosed to the disciples; and the things which were disclosed seem in the sense of the letter so slight as to amount to scarcely anything at all. For the things that are said, and the replies that are given, do not seem to constitute any temptation at all; yet in fact his temptation in the wilderness was more severe than the human mind can possibly comprehend and believe.
>
> All temptation is an attack against the love present in a person, the degree of the temptation depending on the degree of that love. If love is not attacked there is no temptation. Destroying another person's love is destroying his very life, for his love is his life. The Lord's life was love towards the whole human race; indeed it was so great and of such a nature as to be nothing other than pure love. Against this life of his, continual temptations were admitted.
>
> *Arcana Coelestia* 1690

Two Choice Debates with Devils

Of all the debates with devils that occur in the works of Swedenborg two stand out, in my opinion. It is fitting to end this book with them. These final two episodes are paraphrases of the episodes.

Devils are eager to convince angels of heaven that there is no God.

On a certain occasion, some satans in hell were mightily stirred up on the subject of God. As they talked with each other, they honed their arguments that "God" is nothing but an empty word, unless by it one means nature. "If only we could talk to some angels!" they cried. They were burning to overwhelm the angels with their arguments.

Their wish was granted, and while they were emerging from hell, two angels came down from heaven to the world of spirits. The satans were quick to get in the first word, confronting the angels as follows: "People call you wise because you acknowledge God, but oh, how simple you are!" Whereas God cannot be seen, nature can be. "Whose eye can see anything but nature? Whose ear has ever heard anything but nature? . . . Aren't our bodily senses the witnesses of what is true?" And they carried on this theme at length.

The angels heard them out and then said, "You talk in this way because you're engrossed by your senses. All of hell's residents have their thinking immersed in the bodily senses and are unable to raise their minds any higher. So we excuse you."

The angels then put it to them that their minds had been closed to any considerations above the senses, but that being now outside the confining darkness of hell they could understand the way things really are. "You used to live in the natural world," they told them directly, "but you died there and are now in the spiritual world. Did you ever till now know anything about life after death? Haven't you previously denied it?"

The angels explained to them that they were no longer within the realm of nature but above it. And as the angels spelled out their present circumstances, the satans admitted that what the angels said was so. They could grasp it, they said, "in our current state." Later, the satans were given special protection to enable them to endure the aura of heaven.

"They saw magnificent, splendid sights, and because the light of heaven then enlightened them, they acknowledged that there is a God; that nature was created to be subservient to the life that is from God; and that nature in itself is dead and therefore does nothing on its own but is acted upon by life."

That state was only a temporary respite, and as they went downwards and returned to their own lives and favored thoughts, they closed their minds to any light from above.

paraphrase of *True Christian Religion* 77

A highly educated devil argues there is no life after death until at last Swedenborg cannot suppress his laughter.

"What do you do for a living?" That was Swedenborg's question to a satan who was allowed to come up from hell. The answer, spoken with pride, was "the pursuit of learning."

Well then, if he was well-educated, Swedenborg had appropriate questions for him. What did he and his scholarly companions believe about God? He answered that God, heaven, angels, and so on were meaningless terms or ideas held only by ignorant people.

So, what did the academic community he was part of think about religion? Oh, that was a mere flight of imagination. "We believe what we can see and love what we can touch," he said, asserting that the rest was ridiculous nonsense. He laughed at the very concept of heaven and hell. Swedenborg comments, "In saying these things, he spoke precisely as he had thought on the same subjects in the world, not knowing that he was then living after death, since he had forgotten all that he heard on first entering the spiritual world."

And now came a specific question, with an answer too funny for Swedenborg to bear. Is there life after death? The learned spirit began to explain at length why people have had the mistaken notion of life after death. "On hearing this, I could no longer keep from bursting into laughter," we read.

"'Satan,' I said, 'you are raving mad. What are you at this very moment? Don't you have a human shape? Can't you talk, see, hear, walk? Recall that you lived in another world you have forgotten, that you are now living after death, and that you're saying exactly the same things you did before.'

"Then memory returned to him, and he recalled and was ashamed. 'I'm crazy!' he cried. 'I did see heaven up above, and I heard angels there expressing the inexpressible; but that was when I first came here.'"

Paraphrase of *True Christian Religion* 80

This story may be a funny one, but the sad thing is that, having remembered, this highly educated spirit started to forget all the things he did not *want* to remember as he went back down to hell. He resumed his know-it-all attitude and dismissed all that he had just learned as madness. Swedenborg comments, "That is how satans think and talk to each other after death."

Epilogue

As we bring this book to a close, we turn to the closing lines of two of Swedenborg's theological works. The full title of the Swedenborg's book on providence is *Angelic Wisdom Concerning the Divine Providence*. While it is a book of angelic wisdom, we find that devils protest that something should be written from them. Swedenborg has room on the page, and so he writes:

> Forgive me for tacking this on to fill up the rest of the page.
>
> Certain spirits climbed up out of hell by permission. "You've written a lot of things you've received from the Lord," they said to me. "Write a message from us, too."
>
> "What shall I write?" I asked.
>
> "Write that every spirit good or evil enjoys his or her own kind of pleasure—the good the pleasure of their goodness and the evil the pleasure of their evil."
>
> "What is your pleasure?"
>
> "The pleasure of committing adultery, theft, fraud, deceit."

"What are those pleasures like?"

"To others, they come across as the smell of feces or the stink of cadavers or the stench from standing pools of urine."

"But they're pleasing to you?"

"Very!"

"Then you're like the unclean animals that pass their lives in such filth."

"If we are, we are; but those things are perfume to our nostrils."

"What other messages do you want me to write?" I asked.

"Say that everyone is allowed the enjoyment of his or her own pleasure—even the filthiest kind, so called—as long as it doesn't victimize good spirits or angels. But since we can't help making their lives miserable, we're driven away and thrown down into hell, where we endure dreadful torment."

"Why do you inflict misery on the good?"

"We don't have any choice. It's as if a madness takes over whenever we see angels or feel the godly atmosphere around them."

"Then you're nothing more than beasts," I said, at which a madness came over them, a fury presenting itself as a blaze of hatred. To prevent them from causing any harm, they were hauled back into hell.

Divine Providence 340:6,7

The last work that Swedenborg saw through the press was *True Christian Religion*. After all those volumes published over a period of a quarter of a century, Swedenborg brought his crowning work to a close. And again we find that devils chime in with their final challenge:

Afterward I heard a hostile murmur from the lower regions and at the same time the words "Do miracles and we'll believe."

"Aren't the things I've described miracles?" I responded.

"No."

"Then what are miracles?"

"Show us the future, reveal what's to come and we'll have faith."

"The Lord doesn't allow that, because the more people know about the future the less they use their rationality and intellect, their prudence and wisdom. Their faculties slow down and weaken.

"What other miracles shall I do?" I pressed.

"Do the kinds of miracles Moses performed in Egypt," came the cry.

"Maybe you'll harden your hearts at them the way Pharaoh and the Egyptians did."

"We won't."

"Swear to me that you won't dance around a golden calf, that you won't worship it as Jacob's descendants did just one month after they saw Mount Sinai all in flames and heard Jehovah himself speaking from inside the fire—in other words after the greatest miracle of all." (The spiritual meaning of the golden calf is carnal appetite.)

"We won't be like Jacob's descendants," was the answer from below.

But then I heard these words from heaven: "If you don't believe Moses and the prophets—the Lord's Word—miracles won't make you believe, any more than they made the children of Jacob do so in the wilderness. You won't have any more faith than they did when they saw with their own eyes the miracles the Lord himself performed when he was in the world."

True Christian Religion 849

Try as they might, the devils in Swedenborg's books did not manage to get the last word.

Bibliography of Works by Emanuel Swedenborg

Apocalypse Explained. 6 vols. Translated by John Whitehead. 2nd ed. West Chester, Penna: The Swedenborg Foundation, 1994–1998.

Apocalypse Revealed. 2 vols. Translated by John Whitehead. 2nd ed. West Chester, Penna: The Swedenborg Foundation, 1997.

Arcana Coelestia. 12 vols. Translated by John Clowes. Rvd. John F. Potts. 2nd ed.West Chester, Penna: The Swedenborg Foundation, 1995–1998. The first volume of this work is also available under the title *Heavenly Secrets.*

Charity: The Practice of Neighborliness. Translated by William F. Wunsch. Ed. William R. Woofenden. West Chester, Penna: The Swedenborg Foundation, 1995.

Conjugial Love. Translated by Samuel S. Warren. Rvd. Louis Tafel. 2nd ed. West Chester, Penna: The Swedenborg Foundation,

1998. This volume is also available under the title *Love in Marriage,* Translated by David Gladish, 1992.

Divine Love and Wisdom. Translated by John C. Ager. 2nd ed. West Chester, Penna: The Swedenborg Foundation, 1995. This volume is also available in a translation by George F. Dole.

Divine Providence. Translated by William Wunsch. 2nd ed. West Chester, Penna: The Swedenborg Foundation, 1996.

Four Doctrines. Translated by John F. Potts. 2nd ed. West Chester, Penna: The Swedenborg Foundation, 1997.

Heaven and Hell. Translated by John C. Ager. 2nd ed. West Chester, Penna: The Swedenborg Foundation, 1995. This volume is also available in a translation by George F. Dole.

The Heavenly City. Translated by Lee Woofenden. West Chester, Penna: The Swedenborg Foundation, 1993.

Journal of Dreams. Translated by J. J. G. Wilkinson. Introduction by Wilson Van Dusen. New York: The Swedenborg Foundation,1986.

The Last Judgment in Retrospect. Translated by and edited by George F. Dole. West Chester, Penna: The Swedenborg Foundation, 1996.

Miscellaneous Theological Works. Translated by John Whitehead. 2nd ed. West Chester, Penna: The Swedenborg Foundation, 1996. This volume includes *The New Jerusalem and Its Heavenly Doctrine, Earths in the Universe, and The Last Judgment and Babylon Destroyed,* among others.

Posthumous Theological Works. 2 vols. Translated by John Whitehead. 2nd ed. West Chester, Penna: The Swedenborg Foundation, 1996. These volumes include the autobiographical and theological extracts from Swedenborg's letters, additions to *True Christian Religion, The Doctrine of Charity, The Precepts of the Decalogue,* and collected minor works, among others.

True Christian Religion. 2 vols. Translated by John C. Ager. West Chester, Penna: The Swedenborg Foundation, 1996.

Worship and Love of God. Translated by Alfred H. Stroh and Frank Sewall. 2nd ed. West Chester, Penna: The Swedenborg Foundation, 1996.

Collections of Swedenborg's Writings

Conversations with Angels: What Swedenborg Heard in Heaven. Ed. Leonard Fox and Donald Rose. Translated by David Gladish and Jonathan Rose. West Chester, Penna: Chrysalis Books, 1996

A Thoughtful Soul. Translated by and edited by George F. Dole. West Chester, Penna: Chrysalis Books, 1995.

Way of Wisdom: Mediations on Love and Service. Edited by Grant R. Schnarr and Erik J. Buss. West Chester, Penna: Chrysalis Books, 1999

About the Contributors

Donald L. Rose is associate pastor of the Bryn Athyn Society (General Church) and editor of *New Church Life*. A graduate of the Academy of the New Church Theological School, he has lectured on Swedenborg in several countries and pastored churches in the United Kingdom and Australia. He is co-editor of *Conversations with Angels* (1996) and is a member of the Board of Directors of the Swedenborg Foundation.

Lisa Hyatt Cooper translated the passages from Swedenborg's writings that appear in this volume. She is currently translating *Secrets of Heaven* for the New Century Edition of the Works of Emanuel Swedenborg, the first volume of which will appear in 2003. She previously served as primary consultant and American reader on a translation of Swedenborg's *Arcana Caelestia* (London: Swedenborg Society). She has also acted as consultant on several Latin editions of Swedenborg's works and as editor on *De Telluribus*.

Leonard Fox, who contributed the introduction to this volume, is the editor of *Arcana: Inner Dimensions of Spirituality*, a journal devoted to studies in comparative religion and the theology of Emanuel Swedenborg. He co-edited *Conversations with Angels*, and translated and edited Henry Corbin's *Swedenborg and Esoteric Islam* (1994). In addition he has published books on Albanian customary law and grammar, and on Malagasy poetry.

About the Cover

Seeking a cover for a book of this nature was an adventure in itself. The final choice was a picture of unknown date by an unknown artist. It just seemed right, but is it a picture of the devil?

When C. S. Lewis published *The Screwtape Letters* in 1961, the most common question he was asked was whether he actually believed in "the Devil." In response, he wrote the following:

> Now if by "the Devil" you mean a power opposite to God and, like God, self-existent from all eternity, the answer is certainly No. There is no uncreated being except God. God has no opposite. No being could attain a 'perfect badness' opposite to the perfect goodness of God.

Lewis went on to say that we may call "devils" those who by the abuse of their free will have become enemies of God. In the present book, we mean the same thing, whether we say satans, devils or evil spirits. Do they have horns and tails as so often depicted by artists? In their own light, says Swedenborg, they appear to one another as ordinary human beings. In the light of heaven, however, the ugliness of their malice and hatred is revealed in monstrous forms. Horns and tails and cloven feet or gnashing teeth are but visual representations of a person's inward nature. Let the cover suggest in its way a kind of burning that typifies the life of devils.

Also Available from Chrysalis Books

Conversations with Angels, a companion piece to the book you've just read, brings together remarkable selections from Swedenborg's works about the wisdom imparted to him by angels. They reveal their natures, their spiritual loves, their heavenly education, and the true source of wisdom and beauty.

"... an engaging, fascinating contribution to angelic studies."
—REVIEWER'S BOOKWATCH

ISBN: 0-87785-177-8, 176 pages, 8 original illustrations, $12.95

To order this book or receive a catalog of publications, contact Chrysalis Books at 800-355-3222, Ext. 10, or visit our website at www.swedenborg.com